# Key Stage 2
## Numeracy Practice Book Year 3

**Authors**

**Peter Patilla & Paul Broadbent**

EDUCATIONAL

First published 1998
Reprinted 1998 (twice)
Reprinted 1999
This edition 2000

Letts Educational,
9-15 Aldine Street,
London W12 8AW
Tel: 020 8740 2270
Fax: 020 8740 2280

Text © Peter Patilla and Paul Broadbent

Design, page layout and production Moondisks Ltd, Cambridge
Illustrations: Jeffrey Reid, Moondisks
Cover: Ken Vail Graphics

British Library Cataloguing-in-Publication Data
A CIP record for this book is available from the British Library

ISBN 1 84085 057 4

Printed in Spain by Mateu Cromo

Letts Educational Ltd, a division of Granada Learning Limited.
Part of the Granada Media Group.

# Introduction
## to Year 3 Numeracy Practice book

## Numeracy Skills Year 3

This book has been written to develop and improve the numeracy skills of all pupils in Year 3 (ages 7–8).

Each of the ten units of work begins with a double page spread of helpful information. This includes:

- ✓ knowledge needed
- ✓ helpful teaching notes
- ✓ table of what should be learned during the course of the unit

Some pages of activities begin with a Key Skill necessary to complete successfully the activities which follow. Pupils should complete and mark these using the Key Skills answers at the back of the book.

At the end of each unit of work is a summary. This can act both as a quick assessment or as a way to decide which parts of the unit a pupil may omit, or may need to practise further.

# Contents

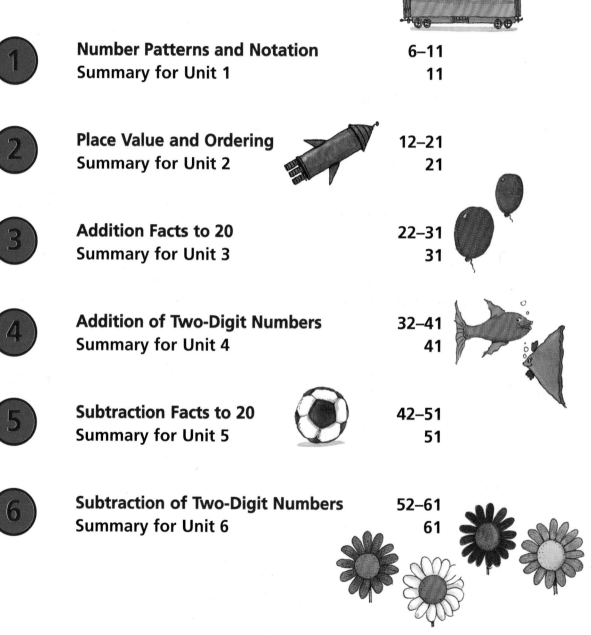

## Knowledge needed
✓ recognising simple odd and even numbers
✓ telling the time
✓ counting on and back in units other than one

# Helpful facts

### Odd and even numbers
All even numbers end in 0, 2, 4, 6 or 8:

even numbers  40, 52, 94, 136, 378

All odd numbers end in 1, 3, 5, 7 or 9:

odd numbers  31, 63, 75, 237, 469

### Important fact
0 is not an even number
Zero means "nothing"
and "nothing" cannot be odd or even

### Multiples
Multiples of 2 are always even:
2, 14, 16, 28, 30, 62, …
Multiples of 5 always end in 5 or 0:
15, 40, 65, 80, …
Multiples of 10 always end in 0:
10, 30, 140, 200, …

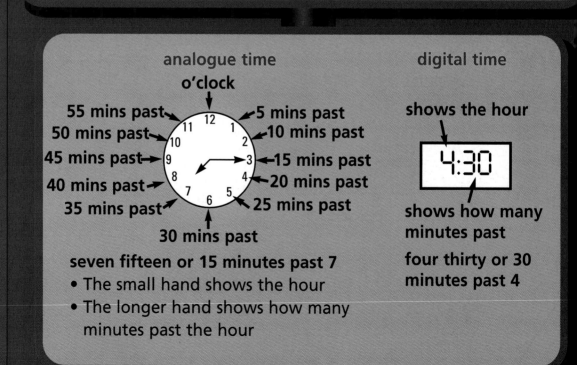

analogue time

o'clock
55 mins past
50 mins past
45 mins past
40 mins past
35 mins past
5 mins past
10 mins past
15 mins past
20 mins past
25 mins past
30 mins past

seven fifteen or 15 minutes past 7
• The small hand shows the hour
• The longer hand shows how many
  minutes past the hour

digital time

shows the hour

4:30

shows how many
minutes past

four thirty or 30
minutes past 4

# Learning outcomes for Unit 1

✓ count on and back in steps of 1, 10 or 100 from any two-digit or three-digit number

✓ count in steps of 3, 4 or 5 from any small number

✓ count on and back in twos and recognise odd and even numbers to about 100

✓ recognise multiples of 2, 5, 10, 100

✓ recognise negative numbers in context

✓ recognise the time using analogue and digital clocks

# Sequences and Patterns

**A**

Copy and write the two missing numbers.

1. 2  4  6  8  ☐ ☐
2. 24  26  28  30  ☐ ☐
3. 38  40  42  44  ☐ ☐
4. 56  58  60  62  ☐ ☐
5. 90  92  94  96  ☐ ☐

6. 17  15  13  11  ☐ ☐
7. 23  21  19  17  ☐ ☐
8. 51  49  47  45  ☐ ☐
9. 75  73  71  69  ☐ ☐
10. 99  97  95  93  ☐ ☐

Write what each group of numbers has in common.

**B**

Write the four missing numbers.

1. ☐ ☐  14  17  20  23  ☐ ☐
2. ☐ ☐   8  13  18  23  ☐ ☐
3. ☐ ☐  13  17  21  25  ☐ ☐
4. ☐ ☐  61  63  65  67  ☐ ☐
5. ☐ ☐  47  57  67  77  ☐ ☐

6. ☐ ☐  46  41  36  31  ☐ ☐
7. ☐ ☐  38  35  32  29  ☐ ☐
8. ☐ ☐  42  38  34  30  ☐ ☐
9. ☐ ☐  72  62  52  42  ☐ ☐
10. ☐ ☐  61  59  57  55  ☐ ☐

**C**

Look at the number machines. Copy and complete the tables.

1.

→ In | +1 | Out →

| In | 46 | | 129 | |
| --- | --- | --- | --- | --- |
| Out | | 54 | | 250 |

2.

→ In | +10 | Out →

| In | 38 | | 190 | |
| --- | --- | --- | --- | --- |
| Out | | 97 | | 300 |

3.

→ In | +100 | Out →

| In | 17 | | 900 | |
| --- | --- | --- | --- | --- |
| Out | | 240 | | 700 |

**D**

Write the number that is the odd one out in each set

1.

46  70  40  58  32  65

2.

15  40  45  35  42  60

3.

20  70  30  50  10  45

# Reading Negative Numbers

**A**

Write the numbers the arrows point to.

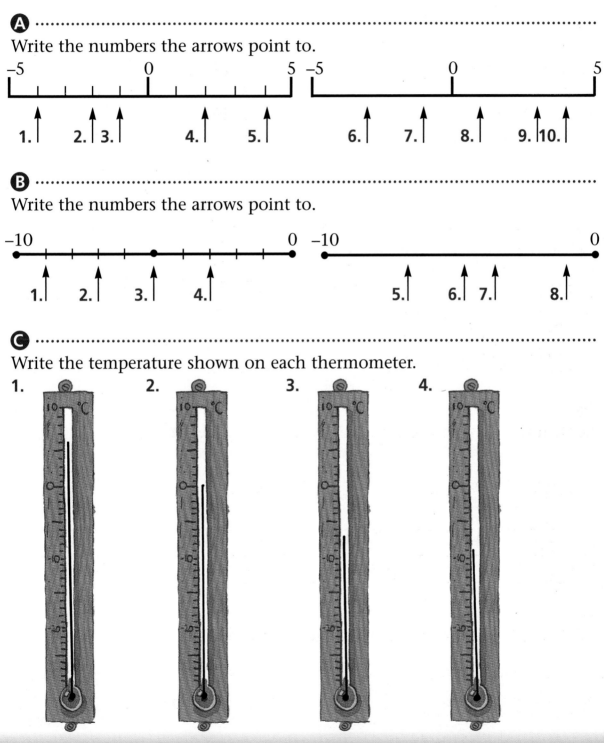

1.  2.  3.  4.  5.  6.  7.  8.  9.  10.

**B**

Write the numbers the arrows point to.

1.  2.  3.  4.  5.  6.  7.  8.

**C**

Write the temperature shown on each thermometer.

1.    2.    3.    4.

9

# Reading Time

**A**

Write the times shown on these clocks.

1.   2.   3.   4.   5.

**B**

Write the times shown on these clocks.

1.   2.   3.   4.   5.

**C**

Write the time one hour later.

1. **4:15**   2. **10:45**   3. **12:30**   4. **6:50**

**D**

Here are some afternoon times.

12:00   5:30   4:55   5:05   4:35   3:50

Write them in order

12:00 ———➔

**E**

Write these afternoon times in order.

**twelve o'clock   six thirty   four fifteen   one o'clock   five thirty**

# Summary for Unit 1

**Ⓐ** ...................................................................................

Write the missing number.

**1.** 23  21  19  17  ☐        **3.** 50  45  40  35  ☐        **5.** 15  12  9  6  ☐
**2.** 24  26  28  30  ☐        **4.** 0  4  8  12  ☐          **6.** 47  49  51  53  ☐

**Ⓑ** ...................................................................................

Write the answers.

**1.** 49 $\xrightarrow{+1}$       **3.** 80 $\xrightarrow{-1}$       **5.** 67 $\xrightarrow{+1}$       **7.** 429 $\xrightarrow{+100}$       **9.** 501 $\xrightarrow{-100}$
**2.** 54 $\xrightarrow{-10}$      **4.** 90 $\xrightarrow{+10}$      **6.** 45 $\xrightarrow{+100}$      **8.** 640 $\xrightarrow{-100}$      **10.** 999 $\xrightarrow{+1}$

**Ⓒ** ...................................................................................

Write the number you estimate each arrow points to.

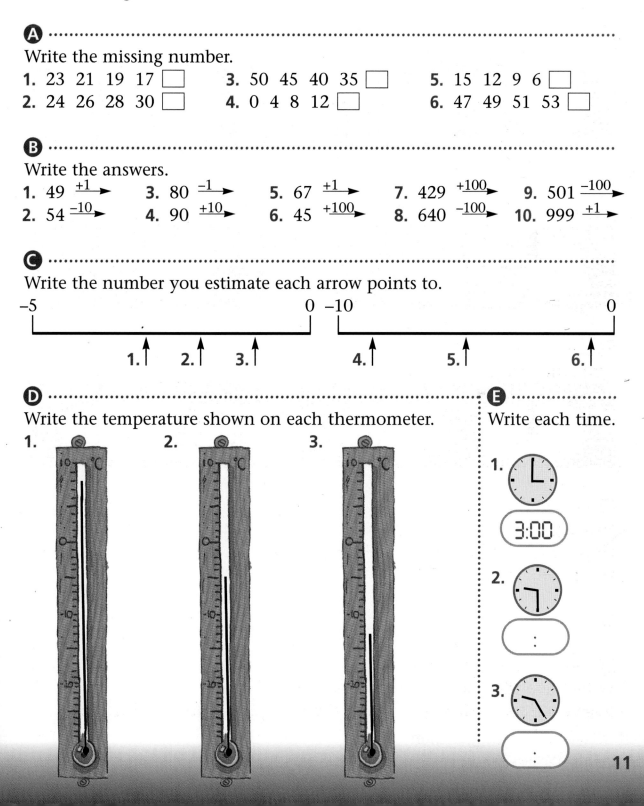

**Ⓓ** ............................................................... **Ⓔ** .......................

Write the temperature shown on each thermometer.      Write each time.

1.        2.        3.

1.  3:00

2.  ⬭

3.  ⬭

11

**Knowledge needed**
- ✓ odd and even numbers
- ✓ using a cm ruler

# Helpful facts

## Two-digit numbers
**These are all the whole numbers from 10 to 99**
tens units

5 6 ——→ 50 + 6

## Number words
**zero, one, two, three, four, five, six, seven, eight, nine, ten, twenty, thirty, forty, fifty, sixty, seventy, eighty, ninety, hundred**

## Three-digit numbers
**These are all the whole numbers from 100 to 999**
hundreds tens units

4 3 7 ——→ 400 + 30 + 7

## Spike abacus
**A spike abacus can be used to show numbers**

hundreds tens units     200 + 10 + 4 = 214

## < and > symbols

> **> means greater than
> or bigger than**    *example*
> 56 > 24

**< means less than
or smaller than**    *example*
227 < 228

# Rounding

- *To the nearest 10*
  look at the last digit;
  if less than 5 round down,
  otherwise round up:

  *examples*
  51 <u>round down</u> ⟩ 50
  163 <u>round down</u> ⟩ 160
  85 <u>round up</u> ⟩ 90
  367 <u>round up</u> ⟩ 370

- *To the nearest 100*
  look at last two digits;
  if less than 50 round down,
  otherwise round up:

  *examples*
  246 <u>round down</u> ⟩ 200
  320 <u>round down</u> ⟩ 300
  450 <u>round up</u> ⟩ 500
  172 <u>round up</u> ⟩ 200

- *To the nearest pound*
  look at the pennies;
  if less than 50p round down,
  otherwise round up:

  *examples*
  £2.49 <u>round down</u> ⟩ £2
  £4.38 <u>round down</u> ⟩ £4
  £1.50 <u>round up</u> ⟩ £2
  £7.84 <u>round up</u> ⟩ £8

# Learning outcomes for Unit 2

✓ read and write numbers to at least 100

✓ know the values of digits in three-digit numbers

✓ know 1, 10 or 100 more than two- and three-digit numbers

✓ compare and order numbers

✓ multiplying and dividing by 10

✓ estimating, approximating and rounding numbers and measures to nearest 10 and 100

✓ use place value in money and measures

✓ vocabulary of number

# Place Value for TU

**A**

1. What does 2 stand for in 42?
2. What does 7 stand for in 79?
3. What does 5 stand for in 15?
4. What does 1 stand for in 12?

5. What does 4 stand for in 94?
6. What does 8 stand for in 87?
7. What does 3 stand for in 83?
8. What does 9 stand for in 98?

**B**

Write what these make.

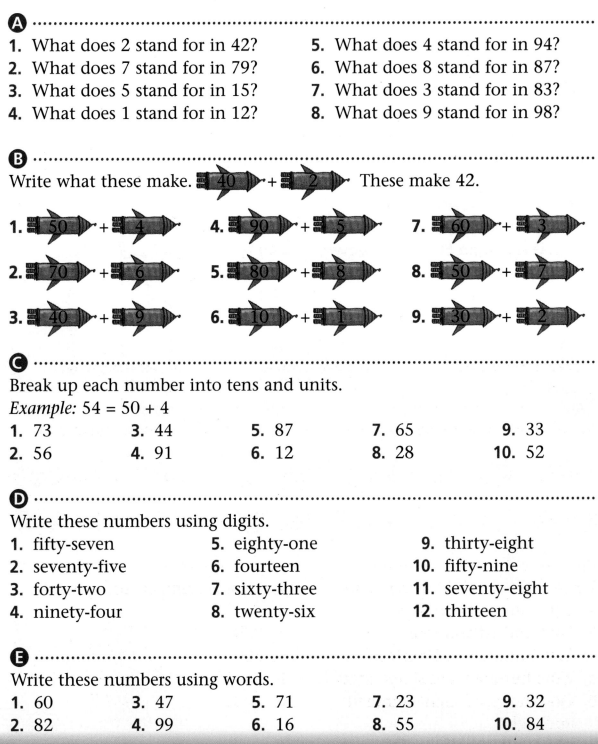

**C**

Break up each number into tens and units.

*Example:* 54 = 50 + 4

1. 73
2. 56
3. 44
4. 91
5. 87
6. 12
7. 65
8. 28
9. 33
10. 52

**D**

Write these numbers using digits.

1. fifty-seven
2. seventy-five
3. forty-two
4. ninety-four
5. eighty-one
6. fourteen
7. sixty-three
8. twenty-six
9. thirty-eight
10. fifty-nine
11. seventy-eight
12. thirteen

**E**

Write these numbers using words.

1. 60
2. 82
3. 47
4. 99
5. 71
6. 16
7. 23
8. 55
9. 32
10. 84

# Place Value for HTU

**A**

Write the value of the underlined digit.

**1.** 32<u>4</u>       **3.** <u>7</u>35       **5.** 14<u>0</u>       **7.** <u>4</u>01       **9.** 10<u>1</u>

**2.** 6<u>5</u>8       **4.** <u>9</u>00       **6.** 9<u>9</u>9       **8.** <u>1</u>23       **10.** 9<u>7</u>2

**B**

Write the number shown on each abacus.

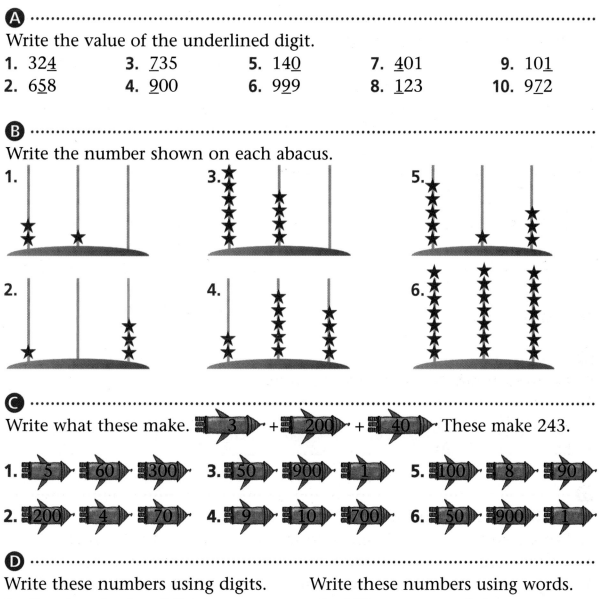

**1.**       **3.**       **5.**

**2.**       **4.**       **6.**

**C**

Write what these make.  3 + 200 + 40  These make 243.

**1.** 5  60  300    **3.** 50  900  1    **5.** 100  8  90

**2.** 200  4  70    **4.** 9  10  700    **6.** 50  900  1

**D**

Write these numbers using digits.       Write these numbers using words.

**1.** One hundred and thirty       **6.** 407

**2.** Six hundred and four       **7.** 720

**3.** Two hundred and thirteen       **8.** 300

**4.** Nine hundred and sixty-eight       **9.** 987

**5.** One thousand eight hundred and eight       **10.** 1025

# Using Place Value

**A** ............................................................................................................

Look at the number machines. Copy and complete the tables.

→ In [ +10 ]Out→

| In | 50 | 65 | 90 | 160 | 990 |
|-----|----|----|----|-----|-----|
| Out |    |    |    |     |     |

→ In [ −10 ]Out→

| In | 84 | 100 | 255 | 400 | 1000 |
|-----|----|-----|-----|-----|------|
| Out |    |     |     |     |      |

**B** ............................................................................................................

Write the number that comes underline{after} these numbers.

**1.** 49      **4.** 648      **7.** 599

**2.** 99      **5.** 319      **8.** 449

**3.** 305     **6.** 800      **9.** 999

Write the number that comes underline{before} these numbers.

**10.** 62     **13.** 249     **16.** 501

**11.** 90     **14.** 720     **17.** 400

**12.** 350    **15.** 305     **18.** 1000

**C** ............................................................................................................

Write each set of numbers in order, starting with the smallest.

**1.**                **2.**                      **3.**

| 64, 46, 58, 42, 60 | 108, 810, 801, 180, 280 | 72 cm, 46 cm, 25 cm, 70 cm, 64 cm |

**D** ............................................................................................................

**1.** Write all the odd numbers between 50 and 60.

**2.** Write all the even numbers which are greater than 61 but less than 73.

**3.** Which even number comes immediately before 100?

**4.** Which of these is an even number when halved? 20, 50, 30, 60, 90.

**E** ............................................................................................................

Write **true** or **false**.

**1.** $56 > 39$      **4.** $104 > 140$      **7.** $97 < 79$      **10.** $650 < 560$      **13.** $45 > 24$

**2.** $84 > 69$      **5.** $950 > 905$      **8.** $80 < 100$      **11.** $94 > 31$      **14.** $245 > 280$

**3.** $30 > 94$      **6.** $38 < 94$      **9.** $420 < 500$      **12.** $60 > 72$      **15.** $317 > 156$

# Estimation of Numbers

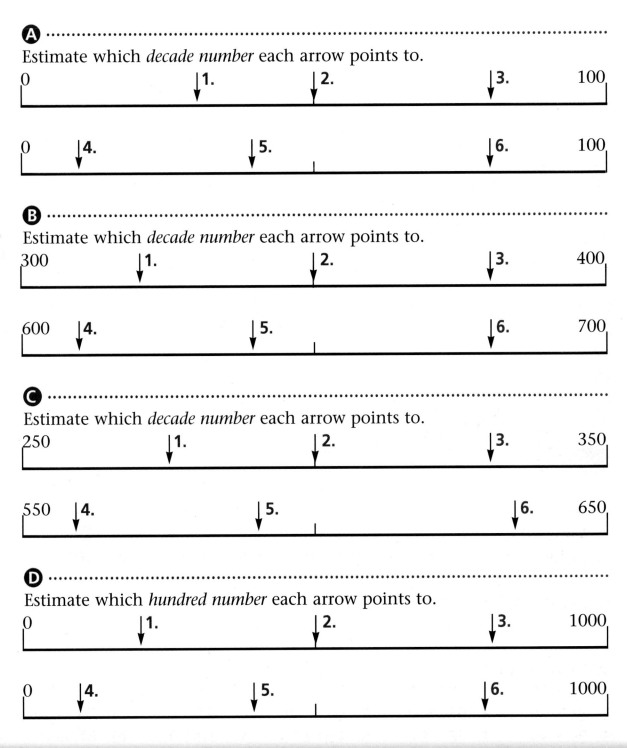

**A**

Estimate which *decade number* each arrow points to.

0            1.         2.              3.           100

0      4.          5.            6.           100

**B**

Estimate which *decade number* each arrow points to.

300          1.         2.              3.           400

600      4.          5.            6.           700

**C**

Estimate which *decade number* each arrow points to.

250          1.         2.              3.           350

550      4.          5.            6.           650

**D**

Estimate which *hundred number* each arrow points to.

0            1.         2.              3.           1000

0      4.          5.            6.           1000

**2.5**

# Approximating Numbers

**A** ·····································································································

Round each number to the nearest 10.

| | | | | |
|---|---|---|---|---|
| **1.** 18 | **3.** 37 | **5.** 45 | **7.** 75 | **9.** 66 |
| **2.** 24 | **4.** 42 | **6.** 63 | **8.** 99 | **10.** 65 |

**B** ·····································································································

Round each number to the nearest 10.

| | | | | |
|---|---|---|---|---|
| **1.** 126 | **3.** 162 | **5.** 207 | **7.** 503 | **9.** 599 |
| **2.** 195 | **4.** 234 | **6.** 321 | **8.** 457 | **10.** 384 |

**C** ·····································································································

Round each number to the nearest 100.

| | | | | |
|---|---|---|---|---|
| **1.** 140 | **3.** 280 | **5.** 790 | **7.** 810 | **9.** 670 |
| **2.** 260 | **4.** 420 | **6.** 630 | **8.** 550 | **10.** 450 |

**D** ·····································································································

Round each number to the nearest 100.

| | | | | |
|---|---|---|---|---|
| **1.** 137 | **3.** 287 | **5.** 456 | **7.** 725 | **9.** 882 |
| **2.** 346 | **4.** 319 | **6.** 664 | **8.** 894 | **10.** 974 |

**E** ·····································································································

Write each amount to the nearest pound.

| | | | | |
|---|---|---|---|---|
| **1.** £1.40 | **3.** £2.64 | **5.** £5.15 | **7.** £2.60 | **9.** £8.52 |
| **2.** £3.80 | **4.** £6.91 | **6.** £7.48 | **8.** £4.23 | **10.** £3.44 |

# Approximating Lengths

**A**

Write the length of each arrow to the nearest cm.

1.

2.

3.

4.

**B**

Measure the length of each line to the nearest cm.

1.

2.

3.

4.

5.

# Place Value and Tens

**A**

Multiply each number by 10.

1. 7  3. 14  5. 27  7. 46  9. 29  11. 50  13. 75  15. 92

2. 8  4. 19  6. 30  8. 43  10. 40  12. 62  14. 86  16. 64

**B**

Divide each number by 10.

1. 80  3. 70  5. 150  7. 370  9. 490  11. 550  13. 790  15. 600

2. 50  4. 240  6. 430  8. 500  10. 300  12. 700  14. 630  16. 710

**C**

Look at the number machine.
Copy and complete the tables.

→ In | ×10 | Out →

1.
| In | 5 | 8 | 14 | 30 | 38 | 50 |
|----|---|---|----|----|----|----|
| Out | | | | | | |

2.
| In | 7 | | 11 | | | 46 |
|-----|---|----|----|----|-----|----|
| Out | | 90 | | 20 | 250 | |

**D**

Look at the number machine.
Copy and complete the tables.

→ In | ÷10 | Out →

1.
| In | 40 | 70 | 160 | 240 | 370 | 800 |
|-----|----|----|-----|-----|-----|-----|
| Out | | | | | | |

2.
| In | 50 | | 130 | | | 60 |
|-----|----|---|-----|----|----|----|
| Out | | 8 | | 22 | 58 | |

# Summary for Unit 2

**A**
......................................................................................

1. What does the 6 stand for in 63?
2. How many tens are in 43?
3. Write eighty-two using digits.
4. Write 51 in words.

**B**
......................................................................................

1. What is the value of the digit in the triangle?   2 ▲3 4
2. How many hundreds are in 634?
3. Write three hundred and two using digits.
4. Write 380 in words.

**C**
......................................................................................

1. Write the whole number that follows 279.
2. Write the whole number that comes before 750.
3. Write these numbers in order.
   304  403  430  340  440
4. Complete the table.

→ In |×10 |Out→

| In  | 56 |    | 132 |     |
|-----|----|----|-----|-----|
| Out |    | 84 |     | 265 |

**D**
......................................................................................

1. Round 236 to the nearest 10.
2. Round 470 to the nearest 100.
3. Round £6.55 to the nearest pound.
4. Estimate which decade number the arrow points to.

0 _____ 100

**E**
......................................................................................

Write the missing number.

1.  24  In |×10 |Out  ☐
2.  ☐  In |×10 |Out  700
3.  200  In |×10 |Out  ☐
4.  ☐  In |×10 |Out  54

## Knowledge needed
✓ confident counting
✓ beginning quick recall of addition facts to 10

# Helpful facts

## Any way round

The order of adding two numbers does not matter:

$3 + 4 = 4 + 3$
$1 + 7 = 7 + 1$
$8 + 5 = 5 + 8$
$3 + 16 = 16 + 3$

## Pairs that total 10

The number pairs which total 10 are very important:

10,0
9,1
8,2
7,3
6,4
5,5

## Extending number bonds

Use your addition bonds to total bigger numbers:

$3 + 4 = 7$
$30 + 40 = 70$
$6 + 2 = 8$
$60 + 20 = 80$

## Adding on small numbers

Adding on small numbers can be done in the head:

$56 + 2 = 58$
$42 + 3 = 45$
$97 + 1 = 98$

## Quick methods

Adding on 10 should be easy:

$27 + 10 = 37$
$42 + 10 = 52$
$64 + 10 = 74$

Adding on 9 **+ 10 then −1:**

$27 + 9 = 36$
$42 + 9 = 51$
$64 + 9 = 73$

Adding on 11 **+ 10 then + 1:**

$27 + 11 = 38$
$42 + 11 = 53$
$64 + 11 = 75$

# Learning outcomes for Unit 3

✓ solve missing number problems in addition

✓ know addition is commutative: 3 + 4 = 4 + 3

✓ addition bonds to 20 learned

✓ know addition can be done in any order

✓ use quick methods, e.g. +10, +9, +11

✓ addition bonds to 10 learned

✓ know addition and subtraction are inverses

✓ use addition facts in money contexts

✓ addition facts to 20 learned

✓ know vocabulary associated with addition

✓ add on small numbers to any two-digit number

✓ extend addition bonds to adding two decade numbers

✓ total more than two single digit numbers

# Addition Bonds to 10

**A**

Write the answers.

| | | | | |
|---|---|---|---|---|
| **1.** 0 + 6 | **5.** 5 + 0 | **9.** 4 + 0 | **13.** 0 + 4 | **17.** 0 + 5 |
| **2.** 2 + 3 | **6.** 1 + 4 | **10.** 8 + 1 | **14.** 2 + 5 | **18.** 1 + 3 |
| **3.** 3 + 1 | **7.** 0 + 9 | **11.** 2 + 1 | **15.** 0 + 7 | **19.** 4 + 3 |
| **4.** 2 + 2 | **8.** 1 + 2 | **12.** 4 + 4 | **16.** 6 + 1 | **20.** 10 + 0 |

**B**

Write the answers.

| | | | | |
|---|---|---|---|---|
| **1.** 4 + 2 | **5.** 1 + 9 | **9.** 4 + 1 | **13.** 3 + 2 | **17.** 2 + 6 |
| **2.** 1 + 5 | **6.** 0 + 10 | **10.** 3 + 4 | **14.** 2 + 5 | **18.** 2 + 8 |
| **3.** 6 + 0 | **7.** 7 + 1 | **11.** 5 + 1 | **15.** 2 + 7 | **19.** 2 + 4 |
| **4.** 1 + 8 | **8.** 6 + 3 | **12.** 7 + 0 | **16.** 3 + 7 | **20.** 6 + 4 |

**C**

Each sum must make 10.
Write the missing number.

| | | | | |
|---|---|---|---|---|
| **1.** 7 + | **3.** 2 + | **5.** 9 + | **7.** 1 + | **9.** 5 + |
| **2.** 8 + | **4.** 3 + | **6.** 4 + | **8.** 10 + | **10.** 6 + |

**D**

Write the answers.

| | | |
|---|---|---|
| **1.** Total 5 and 4 | **6.** 4 add 3 equals | **11.** Total 7 and 7 |
| **2.** Add 3 and 7 | **7.** 6 more than 2 is | **12.** Add 9 and 4 |
| **3.** 4 plus 2 | **8.** Double 4 | **13.** 2 plus 6 |
| **4.** 5 more than 2 | **9.** Sum 4 and 1 | **14.** 8 more than 5 |
| **5.** 3 and 4 makes | **10.** 5 plus 5 equals | **15.** 1 and 3 makes |

# Using Addition Bonds to 10

**A** ..........................................................................................................

Write the missing numbers.

**1.** $5 + \odot = 7$  **4.** $2 + \odot = 9$  **7.** $\odot + 6 = 7$  **10.** $\odot + 2 = 10$  **13.** $2 + \odot = 6$

**2.** $8 + \odot = 10$  **5.** $6 + \odot = 6$  **8.** $\odot + 4 = 4$  **11.** $5 + \odot = 8$  **14.** $\odot + 0 = 3$

**3.** $4 + \odot = 8$  **6.** $\odot + 3 = 6$  **9.** $\odot + 5 = 10$  **12.** $\odot + 1 = 9$  **15.** $9 + \odot = 9$

**B** ..........................................................................................................

Look at the number machines.
Copy and complete the tables.

**1.**   → In | +4 | Out →

| In | 2 | 5 | 4 | 6 |
|---|---|---|---|---|
| Out | | | | |

**2.**   → In | +5 | Out →

| In | | | | |
|---|---|---|---|---|
| Out | 5 | 6 | 9 | 10 |

**C** ..........................................................................................................

Write the answers.

**1.** $2 + 2 + 2$  **4.** $4 + 4 + 2$  **7.** $4 + 2 + 2$  **10.** $3 + 2 + 3$  **13.** $2 + 2 + 6$

**2.** $3 + 3 + 3$  **5.** $5 + 0 + 3$  **8.** $3 + 0 + 7$  **11.** $3 + 4 + 1$  **14.** $6 + 1 + 2$

**3.** $2 + 3 + 1$  **6.** $1 + 6 + 3$  **9.** $5 + 1 + 2$  **12.** $0 + 5 + 2$  **15.** $2 + 2 + 4$

**D** ..........................................................................................................

**1.** How much is in purse A?

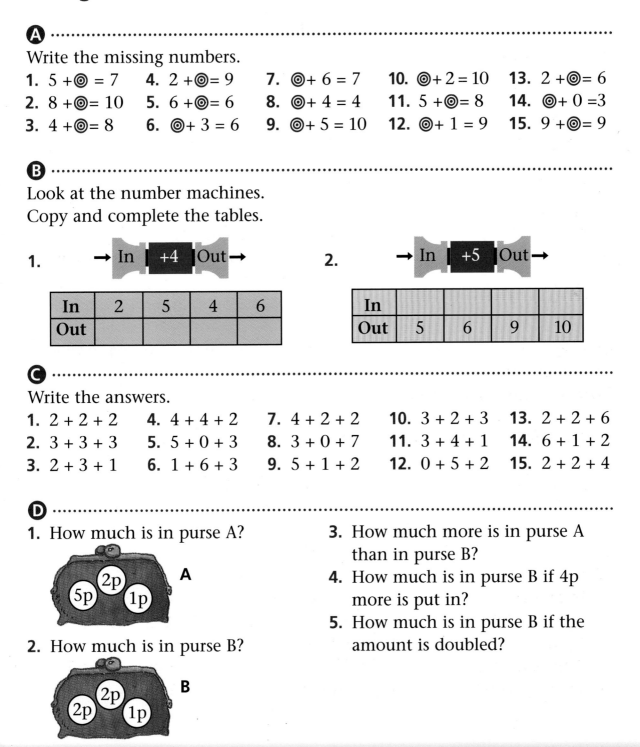

A

**2.** How much is in purse B?

B

**3.** How much more is in purse A than in purse B?

**4.** How much is in purse B if 4p more is put in?

**5.** How much is in purse B if the amount is doubled?

# Addition Bonds 10–15

**A**

Write the answers.

| | | | | |
|---|---|---|---|---|
| **1.** 6 + 5 | **4.** 7 + 6 | **7.** 6 + 6 | **10.** 10 + 2 | **13.** 5 + 7 |
| **2.** 7 + 7 | **5.** 10 + 3 | **8.** 8 + 5 | **11.** 9 + 5 | **14.** 4 + 10 |
| **3.** 4 + 9 | **6.** 7 + 8 | **9.** 6 + 7 | **12.** 7 + 5 | **15.** 5 + 8 |

**B**

Write the answers.

| | | | | |
|---|---|---|---|---|
| **1.** 9 + 2 | **4.** 5 + 6 | **7.** 3 + 9 | **10.** 2 + 9 | **13.** 4 + 8 |
| **2** 10 + 1 | **5.** 7 + 4 | **8.** 8 + 6 | **11.** 3 + 8 | **14.** 6 + 9 |
| **3.** 8 + 3 | **6.** 4 + 7 | **9.** 2 + 10 | **12.** 8 + 7 | **15.** 10 + 4 |

**C**

Write the missing numbers.

| | | | | |
|---|---|---|---|---|
| **1.** $6 \xrightarrow{+7} \blacksquare$ | **4.** $4 \xrightarrow{+7} \blacksquare$ | **7.** $\blacksquare \xrightarrow{+4} 9$ | **10.** $\blacksquare \xrightarrow{+9} 13$ | **13.** $8 \xrightarrow{+6} \blacksquare$ |
| **2.** $9 \xrightarrow{+5} \blacksquare$ | **5.** $7 \xrightarrow{+8} \blacksquare$ | **8.** $\blacksquare \xrightarrow{+5} 15$ | **11.** $10 \xrightarrow{+5} \blacksquare$ | **14.** $\blacksquare \xrightarrow{+8} 15$ |
| **3.** $6 \xrightarrow{+6} \blacksquare$ | **6.** $\blacksquare \xrightarrow{+4} 7$ | **9.** $\blacksquare \xrightarrow{+7} 14$ | **12.** $\blacksquare \xrightarrow{+3} 12$ | **15.** $6 \xrightarrow{+7} \blacksquare$ |

**D**

Copy and complete the chains.

**1.** $5 \xrightarrow{+4} \blacksquare \xrightarrow{+2} \blacksquare \xrightarrow{+2} \blacksquare \xrightarrow{+2} \blacksquare$

**2.** $1 \xrightarrow{+3} \blacksquare \xrightarrow{+3} \blacksquare \xrightarrow{+4} \blacksquare \xrightarrow{+2} \blacksquare$

**3.** $3 \xrightarrow{+0} \blacksquare \xrightarrow{+5} \blacksquare \xrightarrow{+2} \blacksquare \xrightarrow{+3} \blacksquare$

**4.** $0 \xrightarrow{+5} \blacksquare \xrightarrow{+5} \blacksquare \xrightarrow{+2} \blacksquare \xrightarrow{+1} \blacksquare$

**5.** $6 \xrightarrow{+1} \blacksquare \xrightarrow{+2} \blacksquare \xrightarrow{+3} \blacksquare \xrightarrow{+3} \blacksquare$

**6.** $2 \xrightarrow{+3} \blacksquare \xrightarrow{+5} \blacksquare \xrightarrow{+1} \blacksquare \xrightarrow{+3} \blacksquare$

**E**

Ian
10
Today

Lucy
7
Today

Greg
5
Today

**1.** Who is the oldest?
**2.** Who is the youngest?
**3.** Who is twice as old as Greg?
**4.** Who is three years older than Lucy?
**5.** How much older than Greg is Ian?

# Learning outcomes for Unit 4

✓ mentally add any pair of decade numbers

✓ total three or more two-digit numbers

✓ mentally add any digit to a two-digit number

✓ find the complement to total 100

✓ solve missing number problems

✓ double any decade number mentally

✓ total two-digit numbers in the context of money and measures

✓ total decade and two-digit numbers – some mentally

✓ total any pair of two-digit numbers – some mentally

# Adding TU and U

Complete these sums and check your answers.

| | | | | |
|---|---|---|---|---|
| **1.** $7 + 2$ | **3.** $8 + 1$ | **5.** $3 + 4$ | **7.** $6 + 1$ | **9.** $4 + 2$ |
| **2.** $3 + 2$ | **4.** $5 + 4$ | **6.** $2 + 8$ | **8.** $5 + 2$ | **10.** $3 + 7$ |

**A**

| | | | | |
|---|---|---|---|---|
| **1.** $24 + 3$ | **5.** $38 + 1$ | **9.** $54 + 5$ | **13.** $62 + 3$ | **17.** $81 + 8$ |
| **2.** $36 + 2$ | **6.** $42 + 2$ | **10.** $52 + 7$ | **14.** $61 + 5$ | **18.** $88 + 1$ |
| **3.** $21 + 8$ | **7.** $48 + 1$ | **11.** $57 + 2$ | **15.** $70 + 9$ | **19.** $92 + 7$ |
| **4.** $35 + 4$ | **8.** $45 + 4$ | **12.** $68 + 1$ | **16.** $74 + 3$ | **20.** $95 + 4$ |

**B**

| | | | | |
|---|---|---|---|---|
| **1.** $2 + 24$ | **5.** $4 + 52$ | **9.** $6 + 72$ | **13.** $8 + 60$ | **17.** $5 + 42$ |
| **2.** $3 + 36$ | **6.** $5 + 71$ | **10.** $4 + 62$ | **14.** $1 + 57$ | **18.** $4 + 35$ |
| **3.** $1 + 58$ | **7.** $2 + 67$ | **11.** $7 + 81$ | **15.** $9 + 80$ | **19.** $2 + 63$ |
| **4.** $4 + 44$ | **8.** $1 + 58$ | **12.** $3 + 55$ | **16.** $2 + 63$ | **20.** $6 + 93$ |

**C**

| | | | | |
|---|---|---|---|---|
| **1.** $42 + 8$ | **5.** $1 + 69$ | **9.** $74 + 6$ | **13.** $2 + 28$ | **17.** $78 + 2$ |
| **2.** $58 + 2$ | **6.** $3 + 27$ | **10.** $89 + 1$ | **14.** $35 + 5$ | **18.** $8 + 92$ |
| **3.** $61 + 9$ | **7.** $7 + 33$ | **11.** $51 + 9$ | **15.** $8 + 82$ | **19.** $6 + 84$ |
| **4.** $75 + 5$ | **8.** $4 + 64$ | **12.** $65 + 5$ | **16.** $63 + 7$ | **20.** $91 + 9$ |

**D**

**1.**

| + | 5 | 3 | 2 |
|---|---|---|---|
| 43 | | | |
| 52 | | | |
| 35 | | | |

**2.**

| + | 3 | 1 | 2 |
|---|---|---|---|
| 25 | | | |
| 32 | | | |
| 61 | | | |

**3.**

| + | 6 | 5 | 3 |
|---|---|---|---|
| 32 | | | |
| 44 | | | |
| 54 | | | |

# Adding TU and U

Complete these sums and check your answers.

| | | | | |
|---|---|---|---|---|
| **1.** $7 + 7$ | **3.** $9 + 8$ | **5.** $8 + 5$ | **7.** $4 + 7$ | **9.** $5 + 9$ |
| **2.** $5 + 7$ | **4.** $6 + 5$ | **6.** $9 + 9$ | **8.** $8 + 6$ | **10.** $8 + 8$ |

**A**

| | | | | |
|---|---|---|---|---|
| **1.** $36 + 5$ | **5.** $63 + 9$ | **9.** $65 + 7$ | **13.** $39 + 3$ | **17.** $95 + 6$ |
| **2.** $28 + 7$ | **6.** $49 + 8$ | **10.** $29 + 8$ | **14.** $46 + 8$ | **18.** $99 + 4$ |
| **3.** $54 + 9$ | **7.** $78 + 8$ | **11.** $47 + 7$ | **15.** $66 + 6$ | **19.** $96 + 8$ |
| **4.** $45 + 8$ | **8.** $83 + 8$ | **12.** $84 + 9$ | **16.** $45 + 5$ | **20.** $97 + 7$ |

**B**

| | | | | |
|---|---|---|---|---|
| **1.** $5 + 47$ | **5.** $7 + 35$ | **9.** $5 + 38$ | **13.** $7 + 78$ | **17.** $5 + 66$ |
| **2.** $4 + 37$ | **6.** $6 + 25$ | **10.** $9 + 59$ | **14.** $6 + 66$ | **18.** $5 + 89$ |
| **3.** $8 + 23$ | **7.** $3 + 78$ | **11.** $9 + 68$ | **15.** $4 + 79$ | **19.** $9 + 47$ |
| **4.** $9 + 42$ | **8.** $4 + 58$ | **12.** $8 + 34$ | **16.** $3 + 59$ | **20.** $8 + 55$ |

**C**

Copy and complete each number chain.

**1.** $27 \xrightarrow{+4} \square \xrightarrow{+4} \square \xrightarrow{+4} \square$

**2.** $32 \xrightarrow{+8} \square \xrightarrow{+8} \square \xrightarrow{+8} \square$

**3.** $37 \xrightarrow{+5} \square \xrightarrow{+5} \square \xrightarrow{+5} \square$

**4.** $57 \xrightarrow{+7} \square \xrightarrow{+7} \square \xrightarrow{+7} \square$

**D**

Write the missing numbers.

**1.** $27$ In $+\square$ Out $35$

**2.** $42$ In $+\square$ Out $51$

**3.** $35$ In $+\square$ Out $41$

**4.** $58$ In $+\square$ Out $67$

**5.** $64$ In $+\square$ Out $72$

**6.** $73$ In $+\square$ Out $81$

**7.** $67$ In $+\square$ Out $74$

**8.** $38$ In $+\square$ Out $43$

**9.** $56$ In $+\square$ Out $62$

# Addition with Decades

Write the number which must be added to make
each of these total 10 and check your answers.

**1.** 6      **3.** 2      **5.** 5      **7.** 4      **9.** 9
**2.** 3      **4.** 0      **6.** 7      **8.** 8      **10.** 1

## A

Round each number to the next decade.

| | | | | |
|---|---|---|---|---|
| **1.** 12 | **5.** 29 | **9.** 33 | **13.** 64 | **17.** 47 |
| **2.** 48 | **6.** 57 | **10.** 18 | **14.** 22 | **18.** 51 |
| **3.** 76 | **7.** 82 | **11.** 53 | **15.** 75 | **19.** 86 |
| **4.** 91 | **8.** 61 | **12.** 74 | **16.** 99 | **20.** 35 |

## B

Write the answers.

| | | | | |
|---|---|---|---|---|
| **1.** 30 + 40 | **4.** 20 + 70 | **7.** 60 + 30 | **10.** 20 + 50 | **13.** 30 + 30 |
| **2.** 20 + 20 | **5.** 80 + 10 | **8.** 30 + 20 | **11.** 10 + 40 | **14.** 20 + 60 |
| **3.** 50 + 10 | **6.** 40 + 20 | **9.** 40 + 40 | **12.** 70 + 20 | **15.** 30 + 50 |

## C

Write the answers.

| | | | | |
|---|---|---|---|---|
| **1.** 20 + 80 | **4.** 70 + 30 | **7.** 50 + 80 | **10.** 90 + 90 | **13.** 80 + 60 |
| **2.** 30 + 80 | **5.** 80 + 40 | **8.** 70 + 60 | **11.** 40 + 90 | **14.** 90 + 80 |
| **3.** 60 + 60 | **6.** 90 + 70 | **9.** 40 + 70 | **12.** 70 + 80 | **15.** 50 + 60 |

## D

These are parts of till receipts. Write the totals.

**1.** 40p 50p     **3.** 70p 40p     **5.** 90p 40p     **7.** 10p 40p 50p     **9.** 20p 40p 30p

**2.** 50p 70p     **4.** 70p 70p     **6.** 20p 20p 30p     **8.** 60p 10p 20p     **10.** 30p 30p 30p

# Adding TU and Decades

Complete these sums and check your answers.

| | | | | |
|---|---|---|---|---|
| **1.** 9 + 7 | **3.** 6 + 8 | **5.** 7 + 7 | **7.** 30 + 20 | **9.** 60 + 60 |
| **2.** 8 + 5 | **4.** 9 + 3 | **6.** 40 + 20 | **8.** 70 + 80 | **10.** 90 + 30 |

**A** ......................................................................................

| | | | | |
|---|---|---|---|---|
| **1.** 10 + 36 | **4.** 40 + 29 | **7.** 30 + 54 | **10.** 20 + 64 | **13.** 40 + 75 |
| **2.** 30 + 45 | **5.** 50 + 38 | **8.** 80 + 18 | **11.** 80 + 87 | **14.** 60 + 64 |
| **3.** 20 + 62 | **6.** 40 + 57 | **9.** 50 + 62 | **12.** 90 + 54 | **15.** 80 + 39 |

**B** ......................................................................................

| | | | | |
|---|---|---|---|---|
| **1.** 63 + 20 | **4.** 78 + 20 | **7.** 64 + 10 | **10.** 36 + 70 | **13.** 48 + 70 |
| **2.** 48 + 30 | **5.** 46 + 30 | **8.** 31 + 60 | **11.** 48 + 60 | **14.** 54 + 80 |
| **3.** 51 + 10 | **6.** 58 + 20 | **9.** 28 + 60 | **12.** 56 + 90 | **15.** 69 + 60 |

**C** ......................................................................................

Write the totals of these numbers.

**1.** 30 47 10  **2.** 58 20 20  **3.** 50 30 47  **4.** 25 40 30  **5.** 40 50 52

**D** ......................................................................................

1. Paul has 36p.
   Weston has 50p.
   How much do they have
   altogether?

2. Two lengths of wood are 57 cm
   and 80 cm long.
   What is the total length?

3. Cartoon Time lasts 35 minutes.
   Native Watch lasts 40 minutes.
   How long is this altogether?

4. Lisa had 76 stickers.
   She bought two packets.
   One packet had 20 stickers and
   the other had 10 stickers.
   How many stickers does Lisa
   have now?

5. A computer console cost £49.
   The game was £20.
   What was the total cost?

## Adding TU

Complete these sums and check your answers.

1. 40 + 30      3. 30 + 30      5. 50 + 30      7. 30 + 40      9. 20 + 60
2. 20 + 40      4. 60 + 20      6. 60 + 10      8. 40 + 40     10. 70 + 20

**A**

1. 24 + 12      5. 35 + 34      9. 45 + 22     13. 56 + 31     17. 54 + 13
2. 31 + 26      6. 24 + 45     10. 71 + 15     14. 38 + 21     18. 63 + 24
3. 24 + 24      7. 51 + 26     11. 48 + 51     15. 43 + 46     19. 27 + 22
4. 14 + 35      8. 32 + 67     12. 23 + 35     16. 22 + 46     20. 43 + 26

**B**

1. 36 + 72      5. 25 + 91      9. 37 + 81     13. 64 + 91     17. 73 + 81
2. 41 + 63      6. 73 + 84     10. 72 + 64     14. 84 + 85     18. 92 + 96
3. 73 + 52      7. 65 + 44     11. 53 + 42     15. 63 + 63     19. 63 + 84
4. 68 + 61      8. 82 + 82     12. 35 + 72     16. 54 + 72     20. 55 + 63

**C**

Find the missing digits.
Copy and complete the sums.

1.
```
   2 ●
 + 3 6
 -----
   5 9
```
4.
```
   ● 2
 + 3 5
 -----
   8 7
```
7.
```
   5 2
 + ● 5
 -----
   7 ●
```
10.
```
   2 4
 + ● ●
 -----
   4 8
```
13.
```
   ● ●
 + 1 5
 -----
   3 8
```

2.
```
   4 2
 + 2 ●
 -----
   6 5
```
5.
```
   3 7
 + 5 2
 -----
   ● 9
```
8.
```
   2 8
 + 3 ●
 -----
   ● 9
```
11.
```
   5 ●
 + ● 2
 -----
   6 7
```
14.
```
   2 ●
 + 6 3
 -----
   ● 8
```

3.
```
   4 5
 + 3 1
 -----
   7 ●
```
6.
```
   4 ●
 + 4 2
 -----
   ● 4
```
9.
```
   6 4
 + 2 3
 -----
   ● ●
```
12.
```
   ● 4
 + 3 2
 -----
   9 ●
```
15.
```
   5 7
 + ● 1
 -----
   8 ●
```

# Adding TU

Complete these sums and check your answers.
1. 8 + 8
3. 5 + 8
5. 9 + 9
7. 20 + 60
9. 70 + 70
2. 9 + 7
4. 6 + 9
6. 30 + 50
8. 50 + 90
10. 80 + 60

## A

1. 34 + 27
5. 26 + 34
9. 44 + 28
13. 67 + 53
17. 85 + 29
2. 45 + 18
6. 48 + 26
10. 37 + 58
14. 45 + 96
18. 66 + 85
3. 42 + 29
7. 36 + 49
11. 46 + 54
15. 64 + 88
19. 56 + 67
4. 58 + 28
8. 29 + 44
12. 57 + 49
16. 47 + 77
20. 75 + 75

## B

Double each number.
1. 42
3. 25
5. 47
7. 39
9. 67

2. 34
4. 36
6. 45
8. 46
10. 78

## C

Add the numbers in adjacent boxes to
find the number above.

Find the number at the top of each stack.

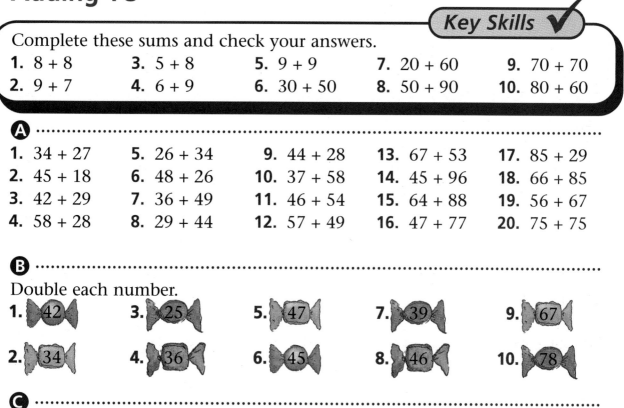

1. 14 26 17
3. 19 25 36
5. 12 41 46
7. 25 32 29

2. 24 36 15
4. 14 35 42
6. 6 40 21
8. 11 49 32

# Addition Problems

Complete these sums and check your answers.

1. 35 + 25   3. 53 + 27   5. 67 + 28   7. 38 + 38   9. 65 + 45
2. 46 + 64   4. 55 + 43   6. 65 + 87   8. 59 + 94   10. 38 + 87

**A** ...................................................................................................

Total these near doubles.

1. 35  34   4. 48  49   7. 34  35   10. 73  72   13. 38  39
2. 46  45   5. 56  55   8. 62  61   11. 75  76   14. 74  75
3. 37  36   6. 47  48   9. 87  86   12. 48  49   15. 85  86

**B** ...................................................................................................

Total these.

1. 56p 44p   3. 27p 75p   5. 55p 45p   7. 38p 38p   9. 29p 87p
2. 36p 85p   4. 68p 72p   6. 87p 15p   8. 65p 64p   10. 66p 66p

**C** ...................................................................................................

Use a number from the first bag.
Add it to a number in the second bag.
Find the total in the third bag.

Find the sums like this.

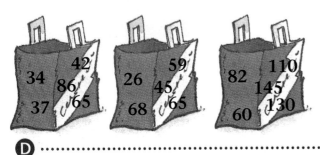

**D** ...................................................................................................

The number in the centre is the total of the three corners.  Find the missing numbers.

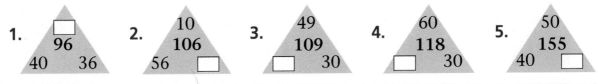

1. □ / 96 / 40  36
2. 10 / 106 / 56  □
3. 49 / 109 / □  30
4. 60 / 118 / □  30
5. 50 / 155 / 40  □

# Summary for Unit 4

**Ⓐ** ...........................................................................................................
| | | | | |
|---|---|---|---|---|
| **1.** 46 + 4 | **3.** 63 + 9 | **5.** 86 + 4 | **7.** 55 + 9 | **9.** 8 + 96 |
| **2.** 5 + 56 | **4.** 8 + 54 | **6.** 93 + 7 | **8.** 7 + 37 | **10.** 7 + 99 |

**Ⓑ** ...........................................................................................................
| | | | | |
|---|---|---|---|---|
| **1.** 30 + 20 | **3.** 50 + 50 | **5.** 90 + 60 | **7.** 25 + 50 | **9.** 80 + 54 |
| **2.** 60 + 20 | **4.** 30 + 80 | **6.** 40 + 36 | **8.** 60 + 54 | **10.** 60 + 83 |

**Ⓒ** ...........................................................................................................
| | | | | |
|---|---|---|---|---|
| **1.** 24 + 35 | **3.** 35 + 45 | **5.** 36 + 27 | **7.** 27 + 37 | **9.** 54 + 29 |
| **2.** 28 + 15 | **4.** 25 + 25 | **6.** 54 + 36 | **8.** 48 + 35 | **10.** 67 + 33 |

**Ⓓ** ...........................................................................................................
| | | | | |
|---|---|---|---|---|
| **1.** 85 + 15 | **3.** 36 + 71 | **5.** 84 + 75 | **7.** 65 + 59 | **9.** 64 + 58 |
| **2.** 47 + 72 | **4.** 96 + 32 | **6.** 63 + 87 | **8.** 78 + 78 | **10.** 67 + 26 |

**Ⓔ** ...........................................................................................................

Each fish must have a value which makes the total 100.
Copy and complete the sums.

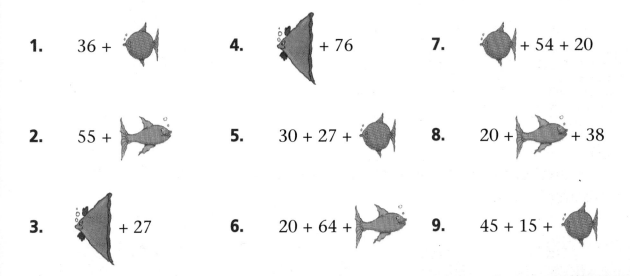

**1.** 36 +

**4.** + 76

**7.** + 54 + 20

**2.** 55 +

**5.** 30 + 27 +

**8.** 20 + + 38

**3.** + 27

**6.** 20 + 64 +

**9.** 45 + 15 +

**Knowledge needed**
- ✓ confident counting forward and back
- ✓ beginning quick recall of facts within 10

# Helpful facts

## Counting on
Sometimes it is efficient to count on when subtracting:

20 – 14

↑

count on from 14 to 20

## Counting back
Sometimes it is efficient to count back when subtracting:

20 – 3

↑

count back 3 from 20

## Difference
To find the number difference between two numbers subtract them:

15        7

the difference between them is $15 - 7 = 8$

## Brackets
When brackets are used, work out the sum in the brackets first:

$12 - (3 + 4)$

↑

work out first

$12 - 7 = 5$

## Extending subtraction bonds
Use subtraction bonds to subtract larger numbers:

$7 - 3 = 4$
$70 - 30 = 40$

# Learning outcomes for Unit 5

✓ subtraction bonds within 10 learned
✓ subtraction bonds within 20 learned
✓ subtraction facts within 20 learned
✓ know addition and subtraction are inverse
✓ extend subtraction bonds to subtracting decades
✓ subtract any small number from any two-digit number
✓ know vocabulary associated with subtraction
✓ use subtraction facts in context of money
✓ solve missing number problems in subtraction
✓ use brackets in simple calculations

# Subtraction Bonds to 10

**A** ......................................................................................

Write the answers.

| | | | | |
|---|---|---|---|---|
| **1.** 8 – 7 | **5.** 8 – 4 | **9.** 9 – 7 | **13.** 6 – 2 | **17.** 10 – 10 |
| **2.** 6 – 3 | **6.** 7 – 4 | **10.** 9 – 4 | **14.** 10 – 7 | **18.** 8 – 2 |
| **3.** 7 – 6 | **7.** 10 – 3 | **11.** 7 – 2 | **15.** 5 – 3 | **19.** 9 – 1 |
| **4.** 10 – 1 | **8.** 9 – 8 | **12.** 10 – 4 | **16.** 7 – 1 | **20.** 10 – 9 |

**B** ......................................................................................

Write the answers.

| | | | | |
|---|---|---|---|---|
| **1.** 9 – 5 | **5.** 6 – 4 | **9.** 10 – 6 | **13.** 9 – 6 | **17.** 9 – 3 |
| **2.** 7 – 5 | **6.** 9 – 9 | **10.** 8 – 5 | **14.** 7 – 3 | **18.** 10 – 8 |
| **3.** 8 – 6 | **7.** 5 – 4 | **11.** 10 – 2 | **15.** 9 – 2 | **19.** 6 – 5 |
| **4.** 10 – 5 | **8.** 5 – 2 | **12.** 8 – 3 | **16.** 4 – 3 | **20.** 10 – 0 |

**C** ......................................................................................

Write the missing numbers.

| | | | | |
|---|---|---|---|---|
| **1.** 8 – ◯ = 3 | **5.** 9 – ◯ = 3 | **9.** ◯ – 2 = 5 | **13.** ◯ – 4 = 4 | **17.** ◯ – 1 = 4 |
| **2.** 6 – ◯ = 4 | **6.** ◯ – 2 = 6 | **10.** ◯ – 5 = 5 | **14.** 10 – ◯ = 7 | **18.** 8 – ◯ = 5 |
| **3.** 10 – ◯ = 8 | **7.** ◯ – 4 = 2 | **11.** ◯ – 4 = 6 | **15.** ◯ – 5 = 2 | **19.** 7 – ◯ = 3 |
| **4.** 8 – ◯ = 5 | **8.** ◯ – 5 = 4 | **12.** 7 – ◯ = 2 | **16.** ◯ – 3 = 6 | **20.** ◯ – 2 = 7 |

**D** ......................................................................................

| | | |
|---|---|---|
| **1.** 6 minus 4 | **4.** 3 less than 7 | **7.** Take away 5 from 9 |
| **2.** 8 take away 5 | **5.** 2 fewer than 6 | **8.** 5 is 3 less than ◯ |
| **3.** 9 subtract 6 | **6.** Subtract 3 from 10 | **9.** ◯ minus 4 leaves 2 |

# Subtraction Bonds to 15

**A** .....................................................................................................

Write the answers.

| | | | | |
|---|---|---|---|---|
| **1.** 14 – 7 | **5.** 13 – 10 | **9.** 15 – 7 | **13.** 15 – 8 | **17.** 11 – 10 |
| **2.** 13 – 8 | **6.** 11 – 4 | **10.** 12 – 9 | **14.** 11 – 9 | **18.** 12 – 5 |
| **3.** 12 – 7 | **7.** 14 – 5 | **11.** 13 – 4 | **15.** 13 – 5 | **19.** 15 – 9 |
| **4.** 11 – 6 | **8.** 11 – 5 | **12.** 12 – 8 | **16.** 14 – 9 | **20.** 13 – 6 |

**B** .....................................................................................................

Write the answers.

**1.** 11 $\xrightarrow{-3}$ ⚽  **5.** 12 $\xrightarrow{-6}$ ⚽  **9.** 11 $\xrightarrow{-7}$ ⚽  **13.** 14 $\xrightarrow{-6}$ ⚽  **17.** 15 $\xrightarrow{-5}$ ⚽

**2.** 13 $\xrightarrow{-7}$ ⚽  **6.** 14 $\xrightarrow{-8}$ ⚽  **10.** 12 $\xrightarrow{-4}$ ⚽  **14.** 13 $\xrightarrow{-3}$ ⚽  **18.** 12 $\xrightarrow{-3}$ ⚽

**3.** 15 $\xrightarrow{-6}$ ⚽  **7.** 11 $\xrightarrow{-1}$ ⚽  **11.** 12 $\xrightarrow{-2}$ ⚽  **15.** 11 $\xrightarrow{-8}$ ⚽  **19.** 13 $\xrightarrow{-3}$ ⚽

**4.** 11 $\xrightarrow{-2}$ ⚽  **8.** 13 $\xrightarrow{-9}$ ⚽  **12.** 15 $\xrightarrow{-10}$ ⚽  **16.** 14 $\xrightarrow{-10}$ ⚽  **20.** 14 $\xrightarrow{-4}$ ⚽

**C** .....................................................................................................

Write the answers.

14  12  13  15  10    12  13  11  14  9    8  13  12  11  14

**1.** Subtract 6 from each number.

**2.** Subtract 4 from each number.

**3.** Subtract 5 from each number.

**D** .....................................................................................................

Work out the sum in the brackets first. Write the answers.

| | | | |
|---|---|---|---|
| **1.** 13 – (10 + 2) | **5.** 15 – (6 + 4) | **9.** 8 – (1 + 4) | **13.** 8 – (2 + 1) |
| **2.** 14 – (3 + 6) | **6.** 10 – (7 + 1) | **10.** 14 – (4 + 8) | **14.** 11 – (6 + 3) |
| **3.** 11 – (6 + 2) | **7.** 13 – (5 + 2) | **11.** 9 – (2 + 2) | **15.** 10 – (1 + 5) |
| **4.** 12 – (4 + 1) | **8.** 15 – (3 + 3) | **12.** 12 – (8 + 1) | **16.** 6 – (2 + 3) |

# Subtraction Bonds to 20

**Ⓐ** .......................................................................................

Write the answers.

| | | | | |
|---|---|---|---|---|
| **1.** 16 – 7 | **5.** 18 – 9 | **9.** 16 – 10 | **13.** 16 – 8 | **17.** 16 – 9 |
| **2.** 15 – 8 | **6.** 16 – 6 | **10.** 18 – 8 | **14.** 19 – 9 | **18.** 18 – 10 |
| **3.** 17 – 10 | **7.** 17 – 9 | **11.** 15 – 9 | **15.** 15 – 7 | **19.** 17 – 7 |
| **4.** 15 – 5 | **8.** 15 – 6 | **12.** 17 – 8 | **16.** 19 – 10 | **20.** 20 – 10 |

**Ⓑ** .......................................................................................

Write the answers.

0          5          10          15          20

| | | | |
|---|---|---|---|
| **1.** 16 — 8 | **5.** — 6 — 9 | **9.** 14 — — 9 | **13.** — 3 — 7 |
| **2.** 17 — 9 | **6.** — 7 — 8 | **10.** 17 — — 8 | **14.** 14 — 6 |
| **3.** 19 — 10 | **7.** — 5 — 7 | **11.** 19 — — 10 | **15.** 16 — 6 |
| **4.** 18 — 9 | **8.** — 8 — 10 | **12.** 20 — — 10 | **16.** — 5 — 8 |

**Ⓒ** .......................................................................................

Work out the brackets first. Answer the sums.

| | | | |
|---|---|---|---|
| **1.** 20 – (6 + 4) | **4.** 17 – (5 + 3) | **7.** 18 – (9 + 1) | **10.** 17 – (8 + 2) |
| **2.** 15 – (6 + 3) | **5.** 16 – (4 + 3) | **8.** 16 – (6 + 2) | **11.** 16 – (5 + 5) |
| **3.** 18 – (4 + 4) | **6.** 17 – (6 + 3) | **9.** 19 – (7 + 2) | **12.** 18 – (8 + 1) |

**Ⓓ** .......................................................................................

**1.** Amy had (20p) and spent 9p. How much change did she have?

**2.** Sandi had (10p)(5p) and had 7p in change. How much did she spend?

**3.** Francis had (10p)(5p)(2p) and spent 8p. How much was left?

**4.** Kim had (5p)(5p)(5p) and bought a 7p chew. How much did she have left?

**5.** Sunil had (5p)(10p)(10p) and spent 6p. How much was left?

**6.** John had (2p)(2p)(10p)(2p) and spent 8p. How much did he have left?

46

# Number Differences

**A**

Write the number differences between the strips on the football scarves.

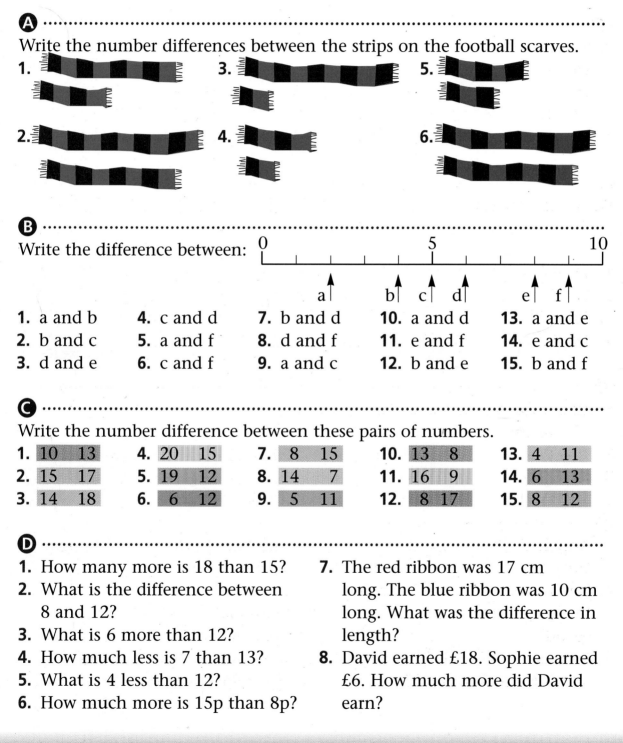

1.

3.

5.

2.

4.

6.

**B**

Write the difference between:

0          5          10

a|    b| c| d|    e| f|

**1.** a and b     **4.** c and d     **7.** b and d     **10.** a and d     **13.** a and e

**2.** b and c     **5.** a and f     **8.** d and f     **11.** e and f     **14.** e and c

**3.** d and e     **6.** c and f     **9.** a and c     **12.** b and e     **15.** b and f

**C**

Write the number difference between these pairs of numbers.

**1.** 10  13     **4.** 20  15     **7.** 8  15     **10.** 13  8     **13.** 4  11

**2.** 15  17     **5.** 19  12     **8.** 14  7     **11.** 16  9     **14.** 6  13

**3.** 14  18     **6.** 6  12     **9.** 5  11     **12.** 8  17     **15.** 8  12

**D**

**1.** How many more is 18 than 15?

**2.** What is the difference between 8 and 12?

**3.** What is 6 more than 12?

**4.** How much less is 7 than 13?

**5.** What is 4 less than 12?

**6.** How much more is 15p than 8p?

**7.** The red ribbon was 17 cm long. The blue ribbon was 10 cm long. What was the difference in length?

**8.** David earned £18. Sophie earned £6. How much more did David earn?

# Teens Subtractions

**A**

Write the answers.

| | | | | |
|---|---|---|---|---|
| **1.** 17 – 2 | **5.** 19 – 5 | **9.** 19 – 7 | **13.** 16 – 0 | **17.** 14 – 2 |
| **2.** 14 – 2 | **6.** 16 – 1 | **10.** 12 – 2 | **14.** 13 – 2 | **18.** 18 – 4 |
| **3.** 18 – 5 | **7.** 19 – 2 | **11.** 19 – 3 | **15.** 18 – 6 | **19.** 17 – 5 |
| **4.** 16 – 3 | **8.** 19 – 4 | **12.** 17 – 3 | **16.** 19 – 6 | **20.** 19 – 8 |

**B**

Copy and complete the tables.

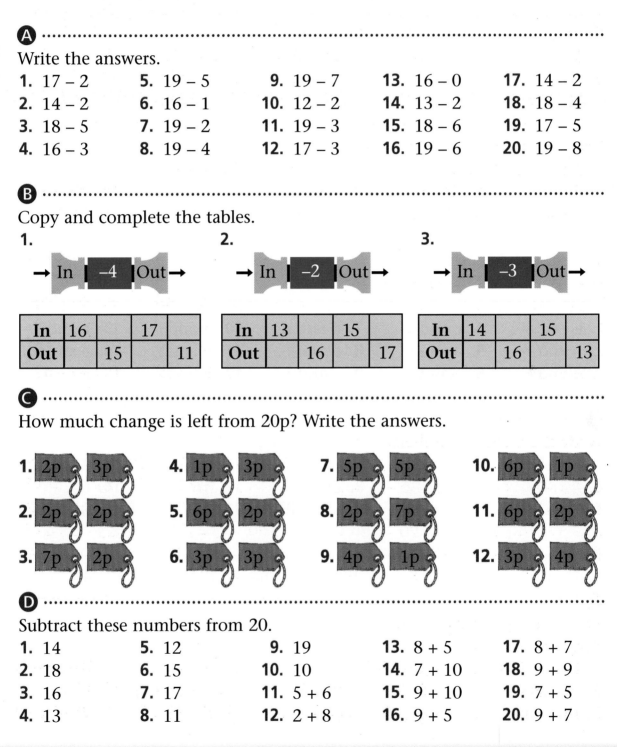

**1.**

→ In | –4 | Out →

| In | 16 | | 17 | |
|---|---|---|---|---|
| Out | | 15 | | 11 |

**2.**

→ In | –2 | Out →

| In | 13 | | 15 | |
|---|---|---|---|---|
| Out | | 16 | | 17 |

**3.**

→ In | –3 | Out →

| In | 14 | | 15 | |
|---|---|---|---|---|
| Out | | 16 | | 13 |

**C**

How much change is left from 20p? Write the answers.

| | | | |
|---|---|---|---|
| **1.** 2p 3p | **4.** 1p 3p | **7.** 5p 5p | **10.** 6p 1p |
| **2.** 2p 2p | **5.** 6p 2p | **8.** 2p 7p | **11.** 6p 2p |
| **3.** 7p 2p | **6.** 3p 3p | **9.** 4p 1p | **12.** 3p 4p |

**D**

Subtract these numbers from 20.

| | | | | |
|---|---|---|---|---|
| **1.** 14 | **5.** 12 | **9.** 19 | **13.** 8 + 5 | **17.** 8 + 7 |
| **2.** 18 | **6.** 15 | **10.** 10 | **14.** 7 + 10 | **18.** 9 + 9 |
| **3.** 16 | **7.** 17 | **11.** 5 + 6 | **15.** 9 + 10 | **19.** 7 + 5 |
| **4.** 13 | **8.** 11 | **12.** 2 + 8 | **16.** 9 + 5 | **20.** 9 + 7 |

## 5.6

# Using Subtraction Facts to 20

Complete these sums and check your answers.
1. $7 - 4$      3. $10 - 3$      5. $15 - 9$      7. $13 - 4$      9. $17 - 3$
2. $8 - 5$      4. $12 - 4$      6. $17 - 8$      8. $6 - 2$      10. $20 - 6$

**Ⓐ**

Use your number facts to answer these.
1. $24 - 2$      4. $46 - 3$      7. $38 - 2$      10. $72 - 1$      13. $77 - 2$
2. $36 - 1$      5. $54 - 2$      8. $19 - 3$      11. $84 - 1$      14. $69 - 4$
3. $28 - 5$      6. $47 - 2$      9. $65 - 4$      12. $75 - 4$      15. $88 - 8$

**Ⓑ**

Use your number facts to answer these.
1. $70 - 40$      5. $50 - 20$      9. $60 - 40$      13. $70 - 50$      17. $60 - 30$
2. $80 - 20$      6. $90 - 50$      10. $80 - 50$      14. $90 - 80$      18. $80 - 30$
3. $60 - 10$      7. $70 - 70$      11. $80 - 60$      15. $80 - 40$      19. $70 - 30$
4. $30 - 20$      8. $50 - 30$      12. $90 - 40$      16. $90 - 70$      20. $90 - 60$

**Ⓒ**

Write the missing numbers.
1. $\bigcirc - 1 = 17$      6. $19 - \bigcirc = 17$      11. $\bigcirc - 3 = 12$      16. $20 - \bigcirc = 18$
2. $\bigcirc - 2 = 11$      7. $15 - \bigcirc = 13$      12. $18 - \bigcirc = 15$      17. $\bigcirc - 2 = 15$
3. $\bigcirc - 4 = 6$      8. $17 - \bigcirc = 13$      13. $\bigcirc - 3 = 13$      18. $16 - \bigcirc = 12$
4. $\bigcirc - 3 = 14$      9. $20 - \bigcirc = 17$      14. $20 - \bigcirc = 19$      19. $\bigcirc - 3 = 16$
5. $\bigcirc - 1 = 18$      10. $18 - \bigcirc = 16$      15. $\bigcirc - 2 = 12$      20. $18 - \bigcirc = 14$

**Ⓓ**

Work out the brackets first.
Answer these sums.
1. $14 - (9 + 4)$      4. $16 - (10 + 2)$      7. $(7 + 9) - 2$      10. $(6 + 9) - 5$      13. $18 - (5 - 4)$
2. $20 - (6 + 4)$      5. $18 - (2 + 3)$      8. $(6 + 5) - 8$      11. $17 - (10 - 3)$      14. $19 - (8 - 4)$
3. $14 - (7 + 7)$      6. $(5 + 8) - 3$      9. $(7 + 7) - 3$      12. $15 - (6 - 2)$      15. $20 - (10 - 3)$

# Subtraction Problems

**A**

1. Two numbers have a difference of 6. The smaller number is 5. What is the larger number?

2. Two numbers have a difference of 5. The larger number is 12. What is the smaller number?

3. Two numbers subtracted leave 14. The larger number is 17. What is the smaller number?

4. Two numbers subtracted leave 3. The smaller number is 9. What is the larger number?

5. Two numbers have a difference of 4. Both numbers are less than 20. One number is double the other. What are the two numbers?

**B**

The highest total wins.   Write who wins in each pair and by how much.

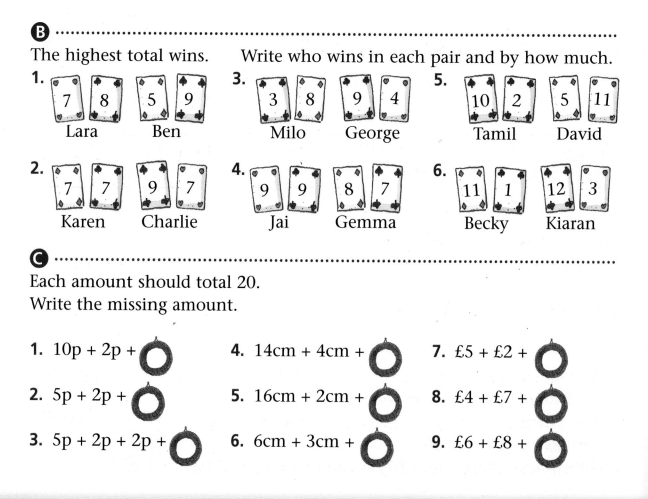

1.
7  8   5  9
Lara      Ben

2.
7  7   9  7
Karen    Charlie

3.
3  8   9  4
Milo     George

4.
9  9   8  7
Jai      Gemma

5.
10  2   5  11
Tamil     David

6.
11  1   12  3
Becky    Kiaran

**C**

Each amount should total 20.
Write the missing amount.

1. 10p + 2p +

2. 5p + 2p +

3. 5p + 2p + 2p +

4. 14cm + 4cm +

5. 16cm + 2cm +

6. 6cm + 3cm +

7. £5 + £2 +

8. £4 + £7 +

9. £6 + £8 +

# Summary for Unit 5

**A** .......................................................................................................

Write the answers.

**1.** 9 – 4     **3.** 10 – 6     **5.** 8 – 4     **7.** 10 – 7     **9.** 8 – 8
**2.** 8 – 2     **4.** 9 – 3     **6.** 10 – 9     **8.** 7 – 5     **10.** 6 – 3

**B** .......................................................................................................

Write the answers.

**1.** 14 – 8     **3.** 12 – 9     **5.** 16 – 7     **7.** 12 – 8     **9.** 15 – 9
**2.** 15 – 7     **4.** 12 – 7     **6.** 11 – 4     **8.** 11 – 8     **10.** 14 – 7

**C** .......................................................................................................

Copy the tables. Write the missing numbers.

**1.**                   **2.**                  **3.**

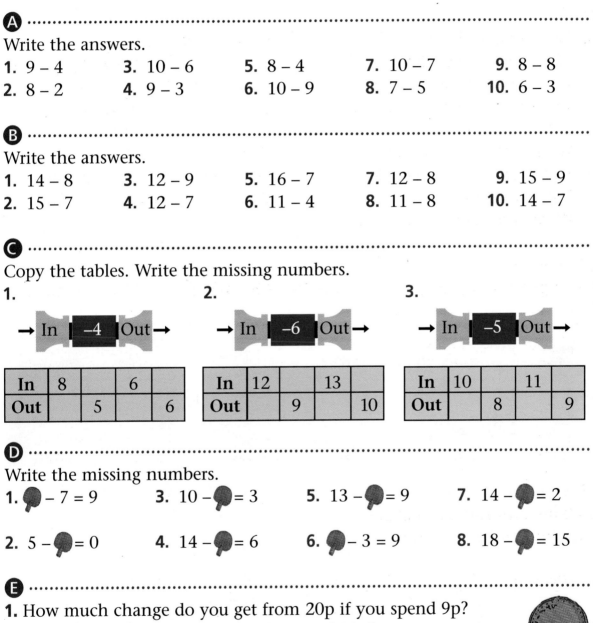

→ In ▮ –4 ▮ Out →     → In ▮ –6 ▮ Out →     → In ▮ –5 ▮ Out →

| In | 8 | | 6 | |
|-----|---|---|---|---|
| Out | | 5 | | 6 |

| In | 12 | | 13 | |
|-----|----|---|----|----|
| Out | | 9 | | 10 |

| In | 10 | | 11 | |
|-----|----|---|----|---|
| Out | | 8 | | 9 |

**D** .......................................................................................................

Write the missing numbers.

**1.** ⬤ – 7 = 9     **3.** 10 – ⬤ = 3     **5.** 13 – ⬤ = 9     **7.** 14 – ⬤ = 2

**2.** 5 – ⬤ = 0     **4.** 14 – ⬤ = 6     **6.** ⬤ – 3 = 9     **8.** 18 – ⬤ = 15

**E** .......................................................................................................

**1.** How much change do you get from 20p if you spend 9p?
**2.** What is the difference between 15p and 19p?
**3.** How much more must be added to 12p to total 20p?
**4.** What is 2p less than 16p?
**5.** What is the change from 20p if you spend 7p and 8p?

51

## Knowledge needed
✓ efficient use of facts within 10
✓ knowledge of tens and units

# Helpful facts

### Brackets
When brackets are used work out the sum in the bracket first:

$(30 + 4) - 3$

↑
work out first

$34 - 3 = 31$

### Quick methods
Subtracting 9
• subtract 10 then add 1:

$28 - 9 = 19$
$64 - 9 = 55$

Subtracting 19
• subtract 20 then add 1:

$52 - 19 = 33$
$65 - 19 = 46$

Subtracting 11
• subtract 10 then 1:

$45 - 11 = 34$
$90 - 11 = 79$

# Learning outcomes for Unit 6

✓ mentally subtract any digit from a two-digit number

✓ mentally subtract any pair of decade numbers

✓ subtract a two-digit number from a decade number – some mentally

✓ subtract any pair of two-digit numbers – some mentally

✓ subtract in the context of money

✓ find the difference between pairs of two-digit numbers

✓ solve missing number problems

# Subtracting TU and U within the Decade

Complete these sums and check your answers.

| | | | | |
|---|---|---|---|---|
| **1.** 9 – 7 | **3.** 7 – 4 | **5.** 5 – 4 | **7.** 8 – 5 | **9.** 8 – 8 |
| **2.** 9 – 5 | **4.** 6 – 2 | **6.** 8 – 7 | **8.** 7 – 3 | **10.** 9 – 6 |

**A** ........................................................................................

Write the answers.

| | | | | |
|---|---|---|---|---|
| **1.** 26 – 4 | **5.** 48 – 6 | **9.** 47 – 5 | **13.** 52 – 1 | **17.** 46 – 3 |
| **2.** 34 – 2 | **6.** 54 – 3 | **10.** 59 – 2 | **14.** 87 – 3 | **18.** 76 – 2 |
| **3.** 25 – 4 | **7.** 65 – 4 | **11.** 77 – 2 | **15.** 63 – 2 | **19.** 95 – 4 |
| **4.** 47 – 1 | **8.** 69 – 5 | **12.** 48 – 5 | **16.** 95 – 2 | **20.** 84 – 3 |

**B** ........................................................................................

| Subtract 4 from each number. | Subtract 3 from each number. | Subtract 5 from each number. | Subtract 6 from each number. |
|---|---|---|---|
| **1.** 38 | **6.** 28 | **11.** 45 | **16.** 21 |
| **2.** 56 | **7.** 46 | **12.** 28 | **17.** 73 |
| **3.** 74 | **8.** 79 | **13.** 39 | **18.** 47 |
| **4.** 59 | **9.** 35 | **14.** 57 | **19.** 62 |
| **5.** 27 | **10.** 67 | **15.** 66 | **20.** 39 |

**C** ........................................................................................

Copy and complete each chain.

**1.** 39 →(−1) →(−4) →(−2)      **4.** 77 →(−1) →(−4) →(−1)

**2.** 48 →(−2) →(−2) →(−2)      **5.** 88 →(−3) →(−2) →(−2)

**3.** 69 →(−3) →(−4) →(−2)      **6.** 59 →(−2) →(−4) →(−1)

# Subtracting TU and U (Crossing the Decades)

**A**

Write the answers.

1. 34 – 7
2. 45 – 8
3. 44 – 7
4. 35 – 9

5. 56 – 8
6. 66 – 7
7. 63 – 6
8. 48 – 9

9. 74 – 6
10. 67 – 9
11. 54 – 8
12. 83 – 7

13. 55 – 7
14. 73 – 5
15. 94 – 5
16. 37 – 8

17. 64 – 9
18. 73 – 4
19. 96 – 9
20. 65 – 6

**B**

Copy and complete the tables.

1.

| – | 2 | 7 | 5 |
|---|---|---|---|
| 41 | | | |
| 71 | | | |
| 81 | | | |

2.

| – | 3 | 6 | 8 |
|---|---|---|---|
| 52 | | | |
| 71 | | | |
| 92 | | | |

3.

| – | 5 | 7 | 9 |
|---|---|---|---|
| 63 | | | |
| 73 | | | |
| 93 | | | |

**C**

Copy and complete the number chains.

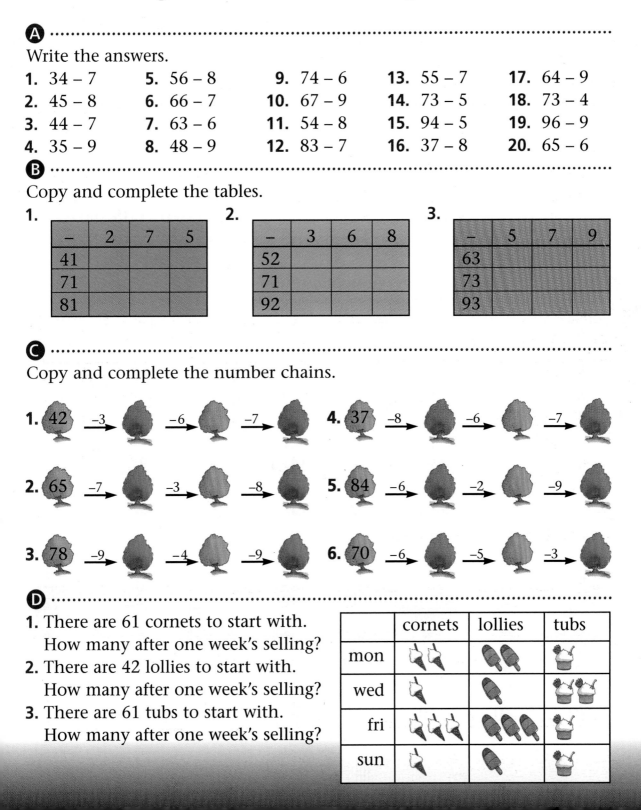

1. 42 –3 → –6 → –7 →
4. 37 –8 → –6 → –7 →
2. 65 –7 → –3 → –8 →
5. 84 –6 → –2 → –9 →
3. 78 –9 → –4 → –9 →
6. 70 –6 → –5 → –3 →

**D**

1. There are 61 cornets to start with. How many after one week's selling?
2. There are 42 lollies to start with. How many after one week's selling?
3. There are 61 tubs to start with. How many after one week's selling?

| | cornets | lollies | tubs |
|---|---|---|---|
| mon | 🍦🍦 | 🍡🍡 | 🍨 |
| wed | 🍦 | 🍡 | 🍨🍨 |
| fri | 🍦🍦🍦 | 🍡🍡🍡 | 🍨 |
| sun | 🍦 | 🍡 | 🍨 |

# Subtracting TU and U (Crossing the Decades)

1. 10 – 5     3. 10 – 4    5. 10 – 8    7. 5 – 3    9. 7 – 4
2. 10 – 9    4. 10 – 7    6. 9 – 4    8. 8 – 6    10. 6 – 3

## A

Write the answers.

1. 30 – 4    5. 90 – 4    9. 90 – 6    13. 30 – 6    17. 90 – 7
2. 50 – 8    6. 50 – 4    10. 60 – 3    14. 40 – 5    18. 80 – 8
3. 30 – 10    7. 40 – 20    11. 80 – 50    15. 70 – 20    19. 90 – 70
4. 60 – 30    8. 70 – 30    12. 90 – 40    16. 60 – 20    20. 80 – 20

## B

Write the missing numbers.

1. 30 – ❀ = 25    6. 90 – ❀ = 83    11. 50 – ❀ = 10    16. 60 – ❀ = 50

2. 80 – ❀ = 71    7. 50 – ❀ = 45    12. 80 – ❀ = 50    17. 80 – ❀ = 10

3. 40 – ❀ = 36    8. 80 – ❀ = 77    13. 40 – ❀ = 20    18. 50 – ❀ = 40

4. 60 – ❀ = 52    9. 70 – ❀ = 69    14. 70 – ❀ = 50    19. 90 – ❀ = 70

5. 70 – ❀ = 68    10. 90 – ❀ = 88    15. 60 – ❀ = 30    20. 70 – ❀ = 30

## C

| Subtract 4 from these. | | Subtract 2 from these. | | Subtract 30 from these. | | Subtract 20 from these. | |
|---|---|---|---|---|---|---|---|
| 1. 40 | 4. 50 | 7. 30 | 10. 90 | 13. 60 | 16. 90 | 19. 50 | 22. 90 |
| 2. 60 | 5. 80 | 8. 70 | 11. 40 | 14. 50 | 17. 70 | 20. 60 | 23. 70 |
| 3. 70 | 6. 30 | 9. 60 | 12. 50 | 15. 60 | 18. 40 | 21. 40 | 24. 80 |

# Subtracting TU from Decades

Complete these sums and check your answers.

1. $42 + ⬤ = 50$
2. $36 + ⬤ = 40$
3. $36 + ⬤ = 40$
4. $68 + ⬤ = 70$
5. $55 + ⬤ = 60$
6. $73 + ⬤ = 80$
7. $64 + ⬤ = 70$
8. $47 + ⬤ = 50$

## A

1. $30 - 15$
2. $40 - 12$
3. $30 - 17$
4. $50 - 11$
5. $40 - 13$
6. $50 - 22$
7. $40 - 24$
8. $50 - 23$
9. $30 - 24$
10. $50 - 34$
11. $40 - 36$
12. $50 - 35$
13. $30 - 26$
14. $40 - 15$
15. $50 - 26$
16. $30 - 19$
17. $40 - 27$
18. $50 - 37$
19. $30 - 11$
20. $40 - 38$

## B

1. $60 - 19$
2. $80 - 38$
3. $70 - 35$
4. $60 - 25$
5. $90 - 23$
6. $70 - 27$
7. $80 - 47$
8. $60 - 28$
9. $90 - 44$
10. $70 - 46$
11. $80 - 54$
12. $90 - 55$
13. $60 - 37$
14. $70 - 38$
15. $80 - 76$
16. $90 - 76$
17. $60 - 46$
18. $80 - 65$
19. $70 - 59$
20. $90 - 62$

## C

Find the missing numbers.

1. $30 - ⬤ = 15$
2. $60 - ⬤ = 24$
3. $40 - ⬤ = 12$
4. $30 - ⬤ = 27$
5. $50 - ⬤ = 31$
6. $70 - ⬤ = 27$
7. $30 - ⬤ = 16$
8. $50 - ⬤ = 29$
9. $60 - ⬤ = 55$
10. $40 - ⬤ = 33$
11. $40 - ⬤ = 24$
12. $90 - ⬤ = 54$

## D

Copy and complete these chain sums.

1. $50 \xrightarrow{-30} \quad \xrightarrow{-4}$
2. $40 \xrightarrow{-20} \quad \xrightarrow{-3}$
3. $50 \xrightarrow{-30} \quad \xrightarrow{-6}$
4. $70 \xrightarrow{-50} \quad \xrightarrow{-8}$
5. $50 \xrightarrow{-40} \quad \xrightarrow{-4}$
6. $80 \xrightarrow{-3} \quad \xrightarrow{-20}$

# Subtracting TU and TU With No Exchange

**Ⓐ** ............................................................................................................

Write the answers.

| | | | | |
|---|---|---|---|---|
| **1.** 36 – 15 | **4.** 39 – 26 | **7.** 36 – 14 | **10.** 54 – 13 | **13.** 27 – 13 |
| **2.** 47 – 24 | **5.** 44 – 21 | **8.** 48 – 25 | **11.** 51 – 21 | **14.** 39 – 29 |
| **3.** 56 – 22 | **6.** 25 – 13 | **9.** 49 – 36 | **12.** 45 – 24 | **15.** 44 – 23 |

**Ⓑ** ............................................................................................................

Write the answers.

| | | | | |
|---|---|---|---|---|
| **1.** 58 – 24 | **4.** 59 – 35 | **7.** 57 – 34 | **10.** 75 – 62 | **13.** 98 – 74 |
| **2.** 63 – 41 | **5.** 74 – 44 | **8.** 77 – 64 | **11.** 84 – 71 | **14.** 72 – 41 |
| **3.** 68 – 52 | **6.** 86 – 62 | **9.** 68 – 34 | **12.** 93 – 63 | **15.** 76 – 34 |

**Ⓒ** ............................................................................................................

Find the difference between:

| | Which number is: | Subtract: |
|---|---|---|
| **1.** 54 ⟿ 12 | **6.** 15 less than 48 | **11.** 14 from 38 |
| **2.** 46 ⟿ 25 | **7.** 25 less than 46 | **12.** 17 from 48 |
| **3.** 37 ⟿ 14 | **8.** 17 less than 59 | **13.** 26 from 59 |
| **4.** 16 ⟿ 38 | **9.** 13 less than 38 | **14.** 34 from 47 |
| **5.** 23 ⟿ 47 | **10.** 24 less than 56 | **15.** 42 from 55 |

**Ⓓ** ............................................................................................................

Work out the brackets first. Answer the sums.

| | | |
|---|---|---|
| **1.** 56 – (10 + 4) | **6.** 47 – (20 – 6) | **11.** (90 – 2) – 24 |
| **2.** 38 – (12 + 3) | **7.** 56 – (20 – 8) | **12.** (60 – 3) – 32 |
| **3.** 47 – (13 + 4) | **8.** 38 – (20 – 6) | **13.** (70 – 5) – 45 |
| **4.** 64 – (12 + 2) | **9.** 65 – (20 – 7) | **14.** (80 – 1) – 56 |
| **5.** 75 – (11 + 2) | **10.** 77 – (20 – 9) | **15.** (60 – 2) – 48 |

## Subtracting TU and TU With Exchange

**A** ··················································································································

**1.** 35 – 18     **5.** 51 – 26     **9.** 52 – 18     **13.** 52 – 28     **17.** 43 – 16

**2.** 42 – 25     **6.** 42 – 26     **10.** 47 – 18     **14.** 43 – 25     **18.** 53 – 25

**3.** 34 – 17     **7.** 46 – 28     **11.** 34 – 15     **15.** 56 – 17     **19.** 44 – 16

**4.** 46 – 19     **8.** 54 – 27     **12.** 58 – 29     **16.** 51 – 37     **20.** 55 – 37

**B** ··················································································

Subtract numbers in **adjacent** bricks to find the number above.
Find the number at the top of each wall.

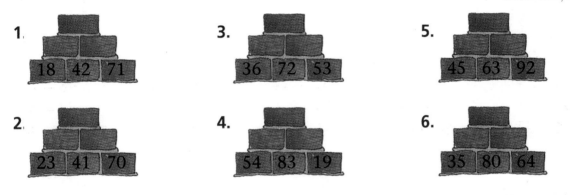

**1.**  18  42  71

**2.**  23  41  70

**3.**  36  72  53

**4.**  54  83  19

**5.**  45  63  92

**6.**  35  80  64

**C** ··················································································

The table shows the number of people walking through the park between 11:00 am and noon.

| Mon | Tue | Wed | Thur | Fri |
|-----|-----|-----|------|-----|
| 16  | 34  | 32  | 50   | 35  |

**1.** How many more people walked on Tuesday than on Monday?

**2.** How many more people walked on Thursday than on Wednesday?

**3.** How many people walked altogether on Monday and Tuesday?

**4.** How many more people walked on Wednesday and Thursday than on Monday and Tuesday?

**5.** What was the difference between Thursday and Friday?

**6.** Which three days totalled 100 people?

# Quick Methods

**A** .......................................................................................

Subtract 9 from each number.

**1.** 28      **3.** 69      **5.** 64      **7.** 31      **9.** 98

**2.** 30      **4.** 46      **6.** 95      **8.** 74      **10.** 52

**B** .......................................................................................

Subtract 20 from each number.

**1.** 43      **2.** 72      **3.** 95      **4.** 86      **5.** 64

Subtract 19 from each number.

**6.** 47      **7.** 58      **8.** 36      **9.** 81      **10.** 74

**C** .......................................................................................

Subtract each number from 100.

**1.** 8      **3.** 12      **5.** 60      **7.** 25      **9.** 72

**2.** 7      **4.** 30      **6.** 14      **8.** 22      **10.** 93

**D** .......................................................................................

This machine subtracts 11 from numbers.
Write the numbers that will leave the machine.

→ In | −11 | Out →

**1.** 43      **4.** 30      **7.** 44      **10.** 58      **13.** 91

**2.** 62      **5.** 89      **8.** 96      **11.** 63      **14.** 74

**3.** 71      **6.** 67      **9.** 35      **12.** 82      **15.** 65

**E** .......................................................................................

How much change would you get from £1?

**1.** 15p

**2.** 37p

**3.** 48p

What is the difference between these pairs?

**4.** 9 and 46

**5.** 7 and 9

**6.** 19 and 36

How much greater is one number than the other?

**7.** 70      43

**8.** 37      60

**9.** 80      11

# Summary for Unit 6

**Ⓐ**
1. 34 – 2
2. 65 – 4
3. 52 – 1
4. 83 – 3
5. 98 – 4
6. 56 – 2
7. 89 – 8
8. 6 – 4
9. 95 – 5
10. 69 – 7

**Ⓑ**
1. 60 – 3
2. 70 – 8
3. 40 – 6
4. 80 – 7
5. 90 – 6
6. 40 – 30
7. 50 – 40
8. 60 – 20
9. 40 – 17
10. 60 – 35
11. 80 – 68
12. 50 – 13
13. 30 – ☐ = 10
14. 70 – ☐ = 68
15. 40 – ☐ = 13

**Ⓒ**
1. 46 – 25
2. 69 – 34
3. 75 – 32
4. 58 – 17
5. 87 – 54
6. What is the difference between 36 and 88?
7. How many more is 94 than 42?
8. How much longer is 83 cm than 41 cm?
9. How much more is £37 than £15?
10. What remains when you subtract 34 from 97?

**Ⓓ**
Write what each box is worth.
1. 56 – ☐ = 49
2. 81 – ☐ = 64
3. 74 – ☐ = 38
4. 65 – ☐ = 37
5. 92 – ☐ = 76
6. 38 – ☐ = 19
7. 45 – ☐ = 28
8. 61 – ☐ = 37
9. 84 – ☐ = 65

**Ⓔ**
Write the missing digits.
1. 36 – 9 = 2●
2. 4● – 9 = 36
3. ●5 – 9 = 54
4. 62 – 9 = ●1
5. 87 – 9 = ●●
6. 76 – 19 = 5●
7. 9● – 19 = 72
8. ●3 – 19 = 24
9. 64 – 19 = ●5
10. 88 – 19 = ●●
11. 100 – ● = 94
12. 100 – 7 = 9●

61

# Helpful facts

## Any way round
The order of multiplication does
not matter:

$2 \times 7 = 7 \times 2$
$5 \times 4 = 4 \times 5$

## Multiplying with 2s
All the answers will be even:

$7 \times 2 = 14$
$2 \times 9 = 18$

## Brackets
When brackets are used, work out
the sum in the brackets first:

$(2 \times 5) - 4$

↑
**work out first**
$10 - 4 = 6$

## Multiplying decade numbers
Multiply the significant numbers
first, then adjust for the tens:

**multiply first**

$2 \times 60 = 120$
$5 \times 70 = 350$

## Multiplying with 5s
All the answers will end with
either 5 or 0:

$7 \times 5 = 35$
$5 \times 6 = 30$

## Multiplying by 10
All the answers will end in 0:

$10 \times 5 = 50$
$6 \times 10 = 60$

## Quick methods
**Multiplying by 4**
• double then double again:

$8 \times 4$
double 16
double again 32

**Multiplying by 5**
• multiply by 10 then halve:

$7 \times 5$
$= \frac{1}{2}$ of $70 = 35$

# Learning outcomes for Unit 7

✓ know 2× and ×2 tables by heart
✓ know 5× and ×5 tables by heart
✓ know 10× and ×10 tables by heart
✓ know 4× and ×4 tables, some by heart
✓ know 3× and ×3 tables, some by heart
✓ know multiplication is commutative:
  $3 \times 4 = 4 \times 3$
✓ recognise multiples of 2, 5 and 10
✓ double numbers
✓ solve missing number problems
✓ use multiplication bonds in context of money
✓ recognise that × and ÷ are inverses

# Multiplying Twos

**A** ....................................................................................................

Write the answers.

1. $4 \times 2$
2. $2 \times 2$
3. $0 \times 2$
4. $3 \times 2$

5. $6 \times 2$
6. $9 \times 2$
7. $7 \times 2$
8. $5 \times 2$

9. $2 \times 10$
10. $8 \times 2$
11. $2 \times 3$
12. $2 \times 4$

13. $2 \times 2$
14. $2 \times 5$
15. $2 \times 0$
16. $2 \times 8$

17. $2 \times 6$
18. $2 \times 10$
19. $2 \times 7$
20. $2 \times 9$

**B** ....................................................................................................

Write the missing numbers.

1. $2 \times \bigcirc = 0$
2. $\bigcirc \times 2 = 10$
3. $2 \times \bigcirc = 4$

4. $4 \times 2 = \bigcirc$
5. $2 \times \bigcirc = 6$
6. $2 \times 4 = \bigcirc$

7. $2 \times 2 = \bigcirc$
8. $\bigcirc \times 2 = 6$
9. $2 \times 5 = \bigcirc$

10. $\bigcirc \times 2 = 20$
11. $6 \times 2 = \bigcirc$
12. $0 \times 2 = \bigcirc$

13. $2 \times 9 = \bigcirc$
14. $7 \times 2 = \bigcirc$
15. $2 \times 8 = \bigcirc$

**C** ....................................................................................................

Look at the number machine.
Copy and complete the tables.

→ In ☐ ×2 ☐ Out →

1.

| In | 5 | 8 | 9 | 7 |
|----|---|---|---|---|
| Out |  |  |  |  |

2.

| In |  |  |  |  |
|----|---|---|---|---|
| Out | 12 | 18 | 16 | 20 |

3.

| In | 3 |  | 6 |  |
|----|---|---|---|---|
| Out |  | 8 |  | 16 |

**D** ....................................................................................................

Use your number facts to answer these.

1. $2 \times 40$
2. $2 \times 80$
3. $2 \times 20$

4. $2 \times 100$
5. $2 \times 50$
6. $2 \times 30$

7. $2 \times 70$
8. $2 \times 10$
9. $2 \times 90$

10. $60 \times 2$
11. $20 \times 2$
12. $40 \times 2$

13. $90 \times 2$
14. $30 \times 2$
15. $10 \times 2$

**E** ....................................................................................................

Work out the brackets first. Answer the sums.

1. $(2 \times 5) - 3$
2. $(7 \times 2) + 4$
3. $(2 \times 8) + 5$
4. $(9 \times 2) - 9$

5. $(6 \times 2) + 8$
6. $30 - (2 \times 2)$
7. $30 - (4 \times 2)$
8. $30 - (2 \times 3)$

9. $30 - (2 \times 6)$
10. $30 - (5 \times 2)$
11. $(2 \times 7) + (2 \times 2)$
12. $(2 \times 9) + (4 \times 2)$

# 7.2

# Multiplying Fives

**A** ............................................................................................................

Write the answers.

| | | | | |
|---|---|---|---|---|
| 1. $5 \times 5$ | 4. $2 \times 5$ | 7. $6 \times 5$ | 10. $9 \times 5$ | 13. $5 \times 0$ |
| 2. $0 \times 5$ | 5. $3 \times 5$ | 8. $8 \times 5$ | 11. $5 \times 2$ | 14. $5 \times 5$ |
| 3. $7 \times 5$ | 6. $4 \times 5$ | 9. $5 \times 10$ | 12. $5 \times 6$ | 15. $5 \times 3$ |

**B** ............................................................................................................

Write the missing numbers.

1. $5 \times 2 = $ ⌣

2. ⌣$\times 5 = 20$

3. ⌣$\times 5 = 10$

4. $5 \times 0 = $ ⌣

5. $5 \times $ ⌣$ = 50$

6. ⌣$\times 5 = 0$

7. $5 \times 3 = $ ⌣

8. ⌣$\times 5 = 15$

9. $5 \times 4 = $ ⌣

10. ⌣$\times 5 = 25$

11. $5 \times $ ⌣$ = 30$

12. $9 \times 5 = $ ⌣

13. $5 \times $ ⌣$ = 10$

14. $6 \times 5 = $ ⌣

15. $5 \times 5 = $ ⌣

16. $10 \times 5 = $ ⌣

**C** ............................................................................................................

⟶ means $\times 5$.  Write the missing numbers.

1. 7 ⟶ ○

2. 4 ⟶ ○

3. 8 ⟶ ○

4. 6 ⟶ ○

5. 9 ⟶ ○

6. ○ ⟶ 40

7. ○ ⟶ 15

8. ○ ⟶ 45

9. ○ ⟶ 25

10. ○ ⟶ 50

11. 5 ⟶ ○

12. ○ ⟶ 35

13. 10 ⟶ ○

14. ○ ⟶ 0

15. 2 ⟶ ○

16. 0 ⟶ ○

**D** ............................................................................................................

Use your number facts to answer these.  Multiply each number by 5.

| | | | | |
|---|---|---|---|---|
| 1. 10 | 3. 30 | 5. 70 | 7. 50 | 9. 60 |
| 2. 40 | 4. 20 | 6. 80 | 8. 90 | 10. 100 |

# Multiplying Tens

**A**
Write the answers.
1. $3 \times 10$  4. $2 \times 10$  7. $10 \times 10$  10. $7 \times 10$  13. $10 \times 2$
2. $5 \times 10$  5. $6 \times 10$  8. $8 \times 10$  11. $10 \times 0$  14. $10 \times 5$
3. $0 \times 10$  6. $4 \times 10$  9. $9 \times 10$  12. $10 \times 4$  15. $10 \times 6$

**B**
Write the missing numbers.
1. $2 \times 10 =$
2. $10 \times 0 =$
3. $3 \times 10 =$
4. $\phantom{0} \times 10 = 0$

5. $10 \times 5 =$
6. $\phantom{0} \times 10 = 40$
7. $10 \times 7 =$
8. $10 \times \phantom{0} = 60$

9. $10 \times 4 =$
10. $\phantom{0} \times 10 = 80$
11. $10 \times 10 =$
12. $10 \times \phantom{0} = 100$

**C**
To multiply by 5 you can multiply by 10 then halve the answer.
Answer these sums.
1. $5 \times 9$  4. $8 \times 5$  7. $5 \times 5$  10. $7 \times 5$
2. $6 \times 5$  5. $5 \times 7$  8. $4 \times 5$  11. $5 \times 3$
3. $5 \times 8$  6. $5 \times 6$  9. $9 \times 5$  12. $5 \times 2$

**D**
Multiply each number by 10.
1. 14  4. 16  7. 36  10. 79  13. 60
2. 17  5. 19  8. 51  11. 40  14. 80
3. 18  6. 25  9. 68  12. 30  15. 70

**E**
$\longrightarrow$ means $\times 10$. Write the missing numbers.

1. $7 \longrightarrow \square$  4. $50 \longrightarrow \square$  7. $120 \longrightarrow \square$  10. $3200 \longrightarrow \square$
2. $14 \longrightarrow \square$  5. $120 \longrightarrow \square$  8. $360 \longrightarrow \square$  11. $9 \longrightarrow \square$
3. $38 \longrightarrow \square$  6. $80 \longrightarrow \square$  9. $500 \longrightarrow \square$  12. $200 \longrightarrow \square$

# Multiplying Twos, Fives and Tens

**A**

Write the answers.

1. $2 \times 3$    5. $5 \times 5$    9. $6 \times 5$    13. $7 \times 10$    17. $8 \times 10$
2. $5 \times 10$    6. $4 \times 5$    10. $2 \times 5$    14. $5 \times 9$    18. $5 \times 7$
3. $5 \times 3$    7. $10 \times 6$    11. $8 \times 5$    15. $8 \times 2$    19. $9 \times 2$
4. $10 \times 4$    8. $2 \times 4$    12. $6 \times 2$    16. $7 \times 2$    20. $5 \times 10$

**B**

Copy and complete the table.

1. $\times 2$

| In | 6 | | 9 | |
|---|---|---|---|---|
| Out | | 14 | | 16 |

2. $\times 5$

| In | 8 | | 10 | |
|---|---|---|---|---|
| Out | | 35 | | 20 |

3. $\times 10$

| In | 9 | | 8 | |
|---|---|---|---|---|
| Out | | 60 | | 50 |

**C**

Work out the brackets first. Answer these sums.

1. $(2 \times 2) + (5 \times 5)$    6. $(6 \times 10) - (2 \times 3)$    11. $(7 \times 2) - (2 \times 5)$
2. $(3 \times 10) + (5 \times 10)$    7. $(9 \times 5) - (2 \times 10)$    12. $(5 \times 5) - (10 \times 0)$
3. $(8 \times 2) + (6 \times 10)$    8. $(10 \times 10) - (3 \times 5)$    13. $(10 \times 6) + (9 \times 2)$
4. $(10 \times 8) + (7 \times 2)$    9. $(7 \times 5) - (6 \times 2)$    14. $(4 \times 2) + (5 \times 9)$
5. $(10 \times 9) + (10 \times 2)$    10. $(2 \times 7) - (0 \times 5)$    15. $(5 \times 4) - (0 \times 2)$

**D**

Calculate the total for each bill.

1. 2 books @ £3
   2 books @ £4

2. 5 stamps @ 30p
   5 stamps @ 50p

3. 10 stickers @ 7p
   10 stickers @ 4p

4. 5 sweets @ 8p
   2 sweets @ 20p

5. 5 drinks @ 10p
   2 drinks @ 20p
   10 drinks @ 30p

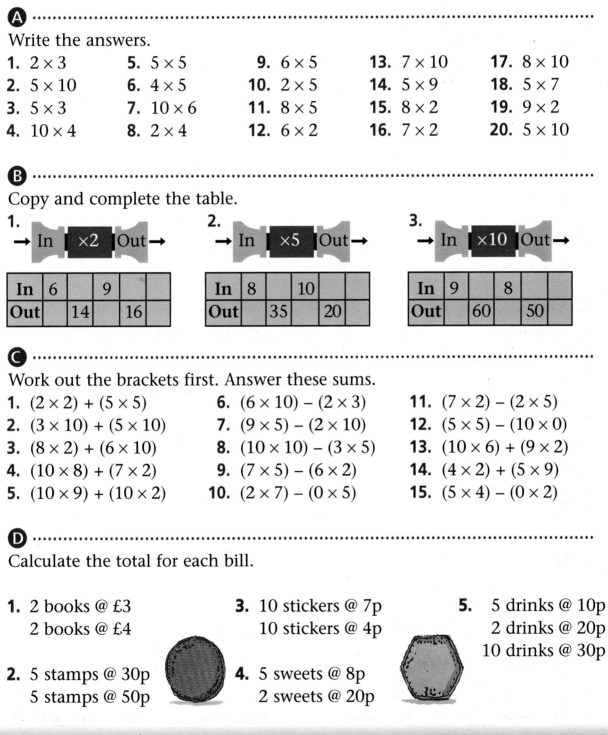

# Multiplying Threes

**A**

Write the answers.

| | | | | |
|---|---|---|---|---|
| **1.** $2 \times 3$ | **5.** $6 \times 3$ | **9.** $9 \times 3$ | **13.** $3 \times 2$ | **17.** $3 \times 9$ |
| **2.** $5 \times 3$ | **6.** $4 \times 3$ | **10.** $7 \times 3$ | **14.** $3 \times 6$ | **18.** $3 \times 10$ |
| **3.** $0 \times 3$ | **7.** $10 \times 3$ | **11.** $3 \times 0$ | **15.** $3 \times 4$ | **19.** $3 \times 7$ |
| **4.** $3 \times 3$ | **8.** $8 \times 3$ | **12.** $3 \times 3$ | **16.** $3 \times 5$ | **20.** $3 \times 8$ |

**B**

Write the missing numbers.

| | | | | |
|---|---|---|---|---|
| **1.** $\bigcirc \times 3 = 6$ | **5.** $\bigcirc \times 3 = 12$ | **9.** $\bigcirc \times 3 = 15$ | **13.** $3 \times 10 = \bigcirc$ | **17.** $7 \times 3 = \bigcirc$ |
| **2.** $3 \times 4 = \bigcirc$ | **6.** $3 \times \bigcirc = 9$ | **10.** $3 \times 9 = \bigcirc$ | **14.** $3 \times 8 = \bigcirc$ | **18.** $\bigcirc \times 3 = 27$ |
| **3.** $0 \times 3 = \bigcirc$ | **7.** $3 \times \bigcirc = 0$ | **11.** $6 \times 3 = \bigcirc$ | **15.** $\bigcirc \times 3 = 30$ | **19.** $3 \times 5 = \bigcirc$ |
| **4.** $3 \times \bigcirc = 3$ | **8.** $3 \times 2 = \bigcirc$ | **12.** $3 \times \bigcirc = 21$ | **16.** $3 \times \bigcirc = 18$ | **20.** $\bigcirc \times 3 = 24$ |

**C**

Use your number facts to answer these.
Multiply each number by 3.

| | | | | |
|---|---|---|---|---|
| **1.** 10 | **3.** 30 | **5.** 50 | **7.** 20 | **9.** 100 |
| **2.** 40 | **4.** 90 | **6.** 60 | **8.** 70 | **10.** 80 |

**D**

1. Kim, Ella and Lee are triplets. They are seven years old. What is the total of their ages?

2. Kelvin has £8 but Pam has three times as much. How much does Pam have?

3. Emily has 27 stickers which is three times as many as George. How many stickers does George have?

4. Moira has three biscuits each day. How many biscuits does she have each week?

# Multiplying Fours

**A** ........................................................................................

Write the answers.

1. $2 \times 4$    **4.** $0 \times 4$    **7.** $9 \times 4$    **10.** $8 \times 4$    **13.** $4 \times 6$
2. $5 \times 4$    **5.** $3 \times 4$    **8.** $10 \times 4$    **11.** $4 \times 2$    **14.** $4 \times 3$
3. $6 \times 4$    **6.** $4 \times 4$    **9.** $7 \times 4$    **12.** $4 \times 0$    **15.** $4 \times 4$

**B** ........................................................................................

Write two different multiplication sums for each number.

1. $\blacksquare \times \blacksquare$ 8 $\blacksquare \times \blacksquare$    **4.** $\blacksquare \times \blacksquare$ 32 $\blacksquare \times \blacksquare$    **7.** $\blacksquare \times \blacksquare$ 40 $\blacksquare \times \blacksquare$

2. $\blacksquare \times \blacksquare$ 12 $\blacksquare \times \blacksquare$    **5.** $\blacksquare \times \blacksquare$ 36 $\blacksquare \times \blacksquare$    **8.** $\blacksquare \times \blacksquare$ 28 $\blacksquare \times \blacksquare$

3. $\blacksquare \times \blacksquare$ 24 $\blacksquare \times \blacksquare$    **6.** $\blacksquare \times \blacksquare$ 18 $\blacksquare \times \blacksquare$    **9.** $\blacksquare \times \blacksquare$ 20 $\blacksquare \times \blacksquare$

**C** ........................................................................................

Here is a number machine. Write the missing numbers. → In █ ×4 █ Out →

1.

| In | 5 | 7 | 8 | 6 | 9 |
|----|---|---|---|---|---|
| Out |  |  |  |  |  |

2.

| In |  |  |  |  |  |
|----|----|----|----|----|----|
| Out | 16 | 36 | 24 | 28 | 40 |

3.

| In | 2 | 4 | 9 |  |  |
|----|---|---|---|----|----|
| Out |  |  |  | 24 | 32 |

**D** ........................................................................................

Use your number facts to answer these.

1. $20 \times 4$    **3.** $30 \times 4$    **5.** $40 \times 4$    **7.** $80 \times 4$    **9.** $10 \times 4$
2. $50 \times 4$    **4.** $70 \times 4$    **6.** $60 \times 4$    **8.** $90 \times 4$    **10.** $100 \times 4$

**E** ........................................................................................

To multiply by 4 you can double then double again.
Try this method and multiply each number by 4.

1. 11    **3.** 12    **5.** 16    **7.** 50
2. 15    **4.** 20    **6.** 30    **8.** 40

# Multiplying with 2, 3, 4, 5 and 10

**A**

Write the answers.

| | | | | |
|---|---|---|---|---|
| 1. $2 \times 9$ | 5. $8 \times 3$ | 9. $8 \times 2$ | 13. $7 \times 4$ | 17. $8 \times 4$ |
| 2. $4 \times 4$ | 6. $7 \times 3$ | 10. $4 \times 9$ | 14. $7 \times 10$ | 18. $8 \times 5$ |
| 3. $5 \times 9$ | 7. $8 \times 10$ | 11. $6 \times 5$ | 15. $6 \times 3$ | 19. $6 \times 2$ |
| 4. $10 \times 9$ | 8. $7 \times 5$ | 12. $2 \times 7$ | 16. $3 \times 9$ | 20. $10 \times 6$ |

**B**

Look at the piles of coins. Write the total amount in each pile.

1. 2p coins          2. 5p coins          3. 10p coins

**C**

Work out the table facts for each tray and total them.
Write the total for each tray. Which tray has the largest total?

1. $4 \times 4$ $3 \times 7$   3. $10 \times 3$ $0 \times 5$   5. $9 \times 5$ $4 \times 4$   7. $3 \times 6$ $5 \times 5$

2. $5 \times 2$ $8 \times 3$   4. $2 \times 9$ $6 \times 5$   6. $2 \times 0$ $5 \times 10$   8. $3 \times 3$ $10 \times 4$

**D**

1. What do four packets of B cost?
2. What do eight packets of C cost?
3. What is the total cost of two packets of D and four packets of C?
4. How much change do you get from £20 if you buy six packets of B?
5. How many packets of A cost the same as four packets of C?

A    £4    B    £3    C    £6    D    £9

# Summary for Unit 7

**A**

1. $6 \times 2 = \square$
2. $2 \times 8 = \square$
3. $2 \times 0 = \square$
4. $\square \times 2 = 18$
5. $2 \times \square = 14$
6. $\square \times 2 = 8$
7. $30 \times 2 = \square$
8. $2 \times 70 = \square$
9. $50 \times 2 = \square$
10. $(2 \times 4) + (9 \times 2) = \square$
11. $(3 \times 2) + (2 \times 10) = \square$
12. $(8 \times 2) - (2 \times 5) = \square$

**B**

1. $5 \times 6$
2. $5 \times 5$
3. $7 \times 5$
4. $6 \xrightarrow{\times 5} \square$
5. $\square \xrightarrow{\times 5} 35$
6. $8 \xrightarrow{\times 5} \square$
7. 5p $\times 4$
8. 5p $\times 8$
9. 5p $\times 6$
10. $100 - (5 \times 8)$
11. $100 - (5 \times 10)$
12. $100 - (5 \times 9)$

**C**

Write the answers.

1. $10 \times 3$
2. $7 \times 10$
3. $4 \times 10$

4. Complete the table.

→ In | ×10 | Out →

| In | 5 | | 10 | | 4 |
|-----|-----|-----|-----|-----|-----|
| Out | | 70 | | 80 | |

How many 10ps in these totals?

5. 50p
6. 30p
7. 70p

**D**

Write the answer.

1. $3 \times 6$
2. $9 \times 3$
3. $4 \times 3$

Write the missing number.

4. $3 \times \underline{\hspace{0.5cm}} = 15$
5. $\underline{\hspace{0.5cm}} \times 3 = 21$
6. $\underline{\hspace{0.5cm}} \times 3 = 24$

Triple each number.

7. 10
8. 40
9. 60

Write what three each of these would cost.

10. 4p
11. 6p
12. 5p

**E**

Write the answer.

1. $4 \times 8$
2. $9 \times 4$
3. $4 \times 7$
4. $5 \times 4$

Write the missing number.

5. $4 \times 6 = \square \times 4$
6. $\square \times 4 = 4 \times 7$
7. $4 \times \square = 10 \times 4$

Write the missing number.

8. $4 \times \square = 20$
9. $\square \times 4 = 32$
10. $\square \times 4 = 24$

Write the answers.

11. $4 \times 40$
12. $4 \times 60$
13. $50 \times 4$

71

## Knowledge needed

✓ multiplication facts for 2, 3, 4, 5, 10x tables

# Helpful facts

### Dividing by two or halving

Dividing by two is the same as halving:

$16 \div 2 = 8$
half of 16 = 8

Halving odd numbers gives an answer with a half in it:

half of $7 = 3\frac{1}{2}$

half of $13 = 6\frac{1}{2}$

### Remainders

These are the remainders possible when dividing by:

| | |
|---|---|
| 2 | 0, 1 |
| 3 | 0, 1, 2 |
| 4 | 0, 1, 2, 3 |
| 5 | 0, 1, 2, 3, 4 |
| 10 | 0, 1, 2, 3, 4, 5, 6, 7, 8, 9 |

### Fractions

$\frac{1}{2}$ is the same as $\div 2$

$\frac{1}{5}$ is the same as $\div 5$

$\frac{1}{10}$ is the same as $\div 10$

$\frac{1}{3}$ is the same as $\div 3$

$\frac{1}{4}$ is the same as $\div 4$

$\frac{1}{2}$ of 12 = 6

$\frac{1}{5}$ of 35 = 7

$\frac{1}{10}$ of 80 = 8

$\frac{1}{3}$ of 12 = 4

$\frac{1}{4}$ of 20 = 5

### Brackets

When brackets are used, work out the sum in the bracket first:

$(21 \div 3) + 4 =$
work out first
$7 + 4 = 11$

### Divisibility

- All even numbers are exactly divisible by 2
- All numbers which end in 5 or 0 are exactly divisible by 5
- All numbers which end in 0 are exactly divisible by 10

# Learning outcomes for Unit 8

✓ know ÷ 2 within table facts by heart
✓ know ÷ 5 within table facts by heart
✓ know ÷ 10 within table facts by heart
✓ know ÷ 3 within table facts, some by heart
✓ know ÷ 4 within table facts, some by heart
✓ know about remainders
✓ relate fractions of quantities to division facts
✓ know multiplication and division are inverses
✓ halve odd and even numbers
✓ solve missing number problems
✓ solve division problems in context of money and measures
✓ round sensibly after a division

# Dividing by 2

**A** ..........................................................................................................

Divide each number by 2. Write the answers.

| | | | | |
|---|---|---|---|---|
| **1.** 4 | **3.** 8 | **5.** 12 | **7.** 10 | **9.** 20 |
| **2.** 2 | **4.** 6 | **6.** 14 | **8.** 18 | **10.** 16 |

**B** ..........................................................................................................

Write how many 2p coins are needed for each amount.

| | | | | |
|---|---|---|---|---|
| **1.** 2p | **3.** 4p | **5.** 8p | **7.** 12p | **9.** 16p |
| **2.** 6p | **4.** 10p | **6.** 14p | **8.** 20p | **10.** 18p |

**C** ..........................................................................................................

Look at the number machine.
Copy and complete the tables.

→ In | ÷2 | Out →

**1.**

| In | 6 | 12 | 20 | 16 |
|---|---|---|---|---|
| Out | | | | |

**2.**

| In | | | | |
|---|---|---|---|---|
| Out | 5 | 9 | 7 | 10 |

**3.**

| In | 6 | | 18 | |
|---|---|---|---|---|
| Out | | 4 | | 8 |

**D** ..........................................................................................................

Use your number facts to answer these.

| | | | | |
|---|---|---|---|---|
| **1.** 20p | **4.** 8p | **7.** 9p | **10.** 19p | **13.** 4 cm |
| **2.** 14p | **5.** 12p | **8.** 11p | **11.** 18 cm | **14.** 16 cm |
| **3.** 16p | **6.** 7p | **9.** 15p | **12.** 10 cm | **15.** 14 cm |

**E** ..........................................................................................................

**1.** Alex and Naomi share 11 marbles between them. How many do they each have?
Is there a remainder?

**2.** Emma and Leslie share 15 pennies between them. How much do they each have?
Is there anything left over?

**3.** David and Sam divide £5 between them. How much do they each have?
Is there any left over?

**4.** Andrea and Gareth divide £13 between them. How much do they each have?
Is there any left over?

# Dividing by 5

**A**

Write the answers.
**1.** 10 ÷ 5　　**3.** 20 ÷ 5　　**5.** 30 ÷ 5　　**7.** 45 ÷ 5　　**9.** 40 ÷ 5
**2.** 5 ÷ 5　　**4.** 15 ÷ 5　　**6.** 25 ÷ 5　　**8.** 35 ÷ 5　　**10.** 50 ÷ 5

**B**

Write the missing numbers.
**1.** ☐ ÷ 5 = 4　**3.** ☐ ÷ 5 = 1　**5.** ☐ ÷ 5 = 5　**7.** ☐ ÷ 5 = 6　**9.** ☐ ÷ 5 = 10

**2.** ☐ ÷ 5 = 2　**4.** ☐ ÷ 5 = 3　**6.** ☐ ÷ 5 = 8　**8.** ☐ ÷ 5 = 7　**10.** ☐ ÷ 5 = 9

**C**

Write how many 5p coins are needed to make these amounts.

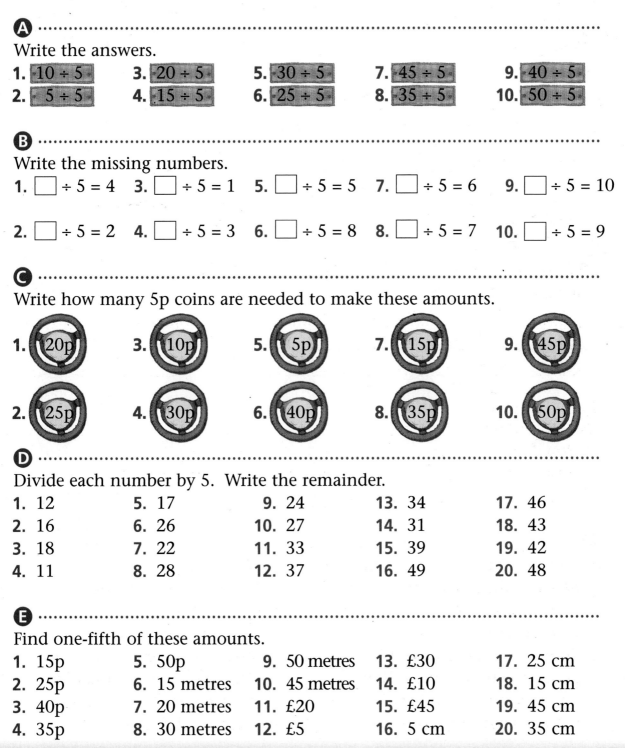

**1.** 20p　　**3.** 10p　　**5.** 5p　　**7.** 15p　　**9.** 45p

**2.** 25p　　**4.** 30p　　**6.** 40p　　**8.** 35p　　**10.** 50p

**D**

Divide each number by 5.  Write the remainder.
**1.** 12　　**5.** 17　　**9.** 24　　**13.** 34　　**17.** 46
**2.** 16　　**6.** 26　　**10.** 27　　**14.** 31　　**18.** 43
**3.** 18　　**7.** 22　　**11.** 33　　**15.** 39　　**19.** 42
**4.** 11　　**8.** 28　　**12.** 37　　**16.** 49　　**20.** 48

**E**

Find one-fifth of these amounts.
**1.** 15p　　**5.** 50p　　**9.** 50 metres　　**13.** £30　　**17.** 25 cm
**2.** 25p　　**6.** 15 metres　　**10.** 45 metres　　**14.** £10　　**18.** 15 cm
**3.** 40p　　**7.** 20 metres　　**11.** £20　　**15.** £45　　**19.** 45 cm
**4.** 35p　　**8.** 30 metres　　**12.** £5　　**16.** 5 cm　　**20.** 35 cm

# Dividing by 10

**A**
Divide each number by 10.  Write the answers.

**1.** 30      **3.** 10      **5.** 60      **7.** 80      **9.** 70
**2.** 40      **4.** 20      **6.** 50      **8.** 90      **10.** 100

**B**
Write the missing numbers.

**1.** ☐ ÷ 10 = 1        **6.** 90 ÷ 10 = ☐        **11.** 40 ÷ 10 = ☐
**2.** ☐ ÷ 10 = 5        **7.** 60 ÷ 10 = ☐        **12.** ☐ ÷ 10 = 7
**3.** ☐ ÷ 10 = 2        **8.** 70 ÷ 10 = ☐        **13.** ☐ ÷ 10 = 8
**4.** ☐ ÷ 10 = 4        **9.** 80 ÷ 10 = ☐        **14.** ☐ ÷ 10 = 6
**5.** ☐ ÷ 10 = 3        **10.** 100 ÷ 10 = ☐      **15.** 50 ÷ 10 = ☐

**C**
Write how many 10p coins in each amount.

**1.** 20p      **3.** 30p      **5.** 70p      **7.** 80p      **9.** 60p

**2.** 40p      **4.** 10p      **6.** 50p      **8.** 90p      **10.** £1

**D**
Divide each number by 10.  Write the remainder.

**1.** 25      **4.** 27      **7.** 56      **10.** 41      **13.** 73      **16.** 92
**2.** 33      **5.** 39      **8.** 42      **11.** 65      **14.** 64      **17.** 87
**3.** 24      **6.** 53      **9.** 58      **12.** 69      **15.** 71      **18.** 98

**E**
Find one-tenth of these amounts.

**1.** 30 cm      **5.** £100      **9.** 40 metres      **13.** 10p
**2.** 80 cm      **6.** £20       **10.** 60 metres     **14.** 60p
**3.** 50 cm      **7.** £40       **11.** 80 metres     **15.** 70p
**4.** 90 cm      **8.** £70       **12.** 70 metres     **16.** 30p

# Dividing by 2, 5 and 10

**A**

1. $6 \div 2$
2. $10 \div 5$
3. $12 \div 2$
4. $50 \div 10$

5. $15 \div 5$
6. $40 \div 10$
7. $20 \div 5$
8. $14 \div 2$

9. $40 \div 5$
10. $60 \div 10$
11. $80 \div 10$
12. $16 \div 2$

13. $45 \div 5$
14. $20 \div 2$
15. $10 \div 10$
16. $35 \div 5$

17. $18 \div 2$
18. $70 \div 10$
19. $50 \div 5$
20. $90 \div 10$

**B**

Copy and write in the missing numbers.

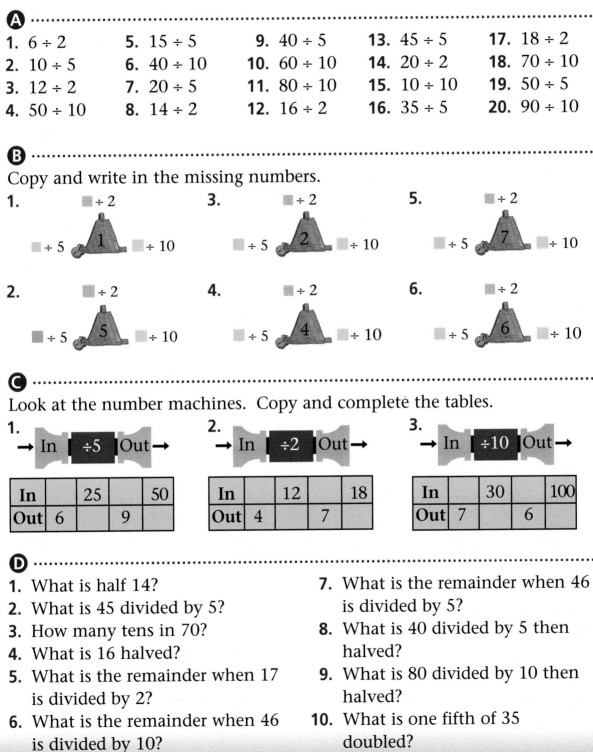

1. ▦ ÷ 2    ▦ ÷ 5    1    ▦ ÷ 10
2. ▦ ÷ 2    ▦ ÷ 5    5    ▦ ÷ 10
3. ▦ ÷ 2    ▦ ÷ 5    2    ▦ ÷ 10
4. ▦ ÷ 2    ▦ ÷ 5    4    ▦ ÷ 10
5. ▦ ÷ 2    ▦ ÷ 5    7    ▦ ÷ 10
6. ▦ ÷ 2    ▦ ÷ 5    6    ▦ ÷ 10

**C**

Look at the number machines. Copy and complete the tables.

1. → In [ ÷5 ] Out →

| In | | 25 | | 50 |
|---|---|---|---|---|
| Out | 6 | | 9 | |

2. → In [ ÷2 ] Out →

| In | | 12 | | 18 |
|---|---|---|---|---|
| Out | 4 | | 7 | |

3. → In [ ÷10 ] Out →

| In | | 30 | | 100 |
|---|---|---|---|---|
| Out | 7 | | 6 | |

**D**

1. What is half 14?
2. What is 45 divided by 5?
3. How many tens in 70?
4. What is 16 halved?
5. What is the remainder when 17 is divided by 2?
6. What is the remainder when 46 is divided by 10?
7. What is the remainder when 46 is divided by 5?
8. What is 40 divided by 5 then halved?
9. What is 80 divided by 10 then halved?
10. What is one fifth of 35 doubled?

# Dividing by 3

**A**

Write the answers. Write how many threes are in numbers 10 to 15.

1. 9 ÷ 3
2. 3 ÷ 3
3. 6 ÷ 3
4. 18 ÷ 3
5. 12 ÷ 3
6. 15 ÷ 3
7. 24 ÷ 3
8. 21 ÷ 3
9. 30 ÷ 3
10. 27
11. 9
12. 12
13. 3
14. 6
15. 18

**B**

Write the missing numbers.

1. ◯ ÷ 3 = 1
2. ◯ ÷ 3 = 4
3. ◯ ÷ 3 = 2
4. ◯ ÷ 3 = 5
5. ◯ ÷ 3 = 3
6. ◯ ÷ 3 = 6
7. ◯ ÷ 3 = 10
8. ◯ ÷ 3 = 7
9. ◯ ÷ 3 = 8
10. ◯ ÷ 3 = 9
11. 0 ÷ 3 = ◯
12. 9 ÷ 3 = ◯
13. 3 ÷ 3 = ◯
14. 15 ÷ 3 = ◯
15. 3 ÷ 1 = ◯

**C**

Divide each number by 3 and write the remainder.

1. 4
2. 8
3. 5
4. 10
5. 7
6. 11
7. 16
8. 13
9. 14
10. 17
11. 19
12. 22
13. 20
14. 23
15. 21

**D**

Look at the number machine.
Copy and complete the tables.

→ In | ÷3 | Out →

**1.**

| In | 21 | 27 | 15 | 24 | 30 |
|---|---|---|---|---|---|
| Out | | | | | |

**2.**

| In | | | | | |
|---|---|---|---|---|---|
| Out | 4 | 8 | 7 | 3 | 9 |

**3.**

| In | 30 | | 18 | | 12 |
|---|---|---|---|---|---|
| Out | | 4 | | 3 | |

**E**

Work out the brackets first. Answer these sums.

1. (21 ÷ 3) + (15 ÷ 3)
2. (12 ÷ 3) + (24 ÷ 3)
3. (9 ÷ 3) + (3 ÷ 3)
4. (27 ÷ 3) + (6 ÷ 3)
5. (18 ÷ 3) + (30 ÷ 3)
6. (30 ÷ 3) – (6 ÷ 3)
7. (24 ÷ 3) – (12 ÷ 3)
8. (21 ÷ 3) – (15 ÷ 3)
9. (27 ÷ 3) – (9 ÷ 3)
10. (18 ÷ 3) – (3 ÷ 3)
11. (21 ÷ 3) x (6 ÷ 3)
12. (24 ÷ 3) x (9 ÷ 3)

# Dividing by 4

**A** ........................................................................................

Divide each number by 4.

| | | | | |
|---|---|---|---|---|
| 1. 4 | 4. 8 | 7. 16 | 10. 40 | 13. 24 |
| 2. 12 | 5. 32 | 8. 36 | 11. 12 | 14. 16 |
| 3. 20 | 6. 24 | 9. 28 | 12. 44 | 15. 48 |

**B** ........................................................................................

Find one-quarter of each number.

Each number is a quarter.
Write the whole amount.

| | | | | |
|---|---|---|---|---|
| 1. 12 | 4. 24 | 7. 36 | 10. 5 | 13. 6 |
| 2. 20 | 5. 8 | 8. 40 | 11. 2 | 14. 4 |
| 3. 4 | 6. 16 | 9. 28 | 12. 1 | 15. 10 |

**C** ........................................................................................

Divide each number by 4 and write the remainder.

| | | | | |
|---|---|---|---|---|
| 1. 9 | 4. 13 | 7. 25 | 10. 22 | 13. 32 |
| 2. 11 | 5. 16 | 8. 23 | 11. 26 | 14. 31 |
| 3. 15 | 6. 21 | 9. 27 | 12. 30 | 15. 29 |

**D** ........................................................................................

Write the missing numbers.

1. $\square \div 4 = 1$    4. $\square \div 4 = 7$    7. $\square \div 4 = 5$    10. $\square \div 4 = 9$    13. $4 \div 4 = \square$

2. $\square \div 4 = 4$    5. $\square \div 4 = 6$    8. $\square \div 4 = 10$    11. $8 \div 4 = \square$    14. $40 \div 4 = \square$

3. $\square \div 4 = 2$    6. $\square \div 4 = 3$    9. $\square \div 4 = 8$    12. $20 \div 4 = \square$    15. $12 \div 4 = \square$

**E** ........................................................................................

1. £24 is shared equally between four children. How much does each child receive?

2. What is one-quarter of £20?

3. Four books cost £12. Each book is the same price. What does each book cost?

4. 36 cm of ribbon is cut into four equal pieces. How long is each piece?

5. What is one-quarter of 32 cm?

6. Four straws the same length are placed end to end. The total length is 40 cm. How long is each straw?

# Dividing by 2, 3, 4, 5 and 10

**A**

Write the answers.

**1.** 18 ÷ 2     **4.** 15 ÷ 3     **7.** 16 ÷ 2     **10.** 35 ÷ 5     **13.** 24 ÷ 4

**2.** 15 ÷ 5     **5.** 36 ÷ 4     **8.** 50 ÷ 10     **11.** 14 ÷ 2     **14.** 24 ÷ 3

**3.** 30 ÷ 10     **6.** 21 ÷ 3     **9.** 16 ÷ 4     **12.** 45 ÷ 5     **15.** 70 ÷ 10

**B**

Copy and write in the missing numbers.

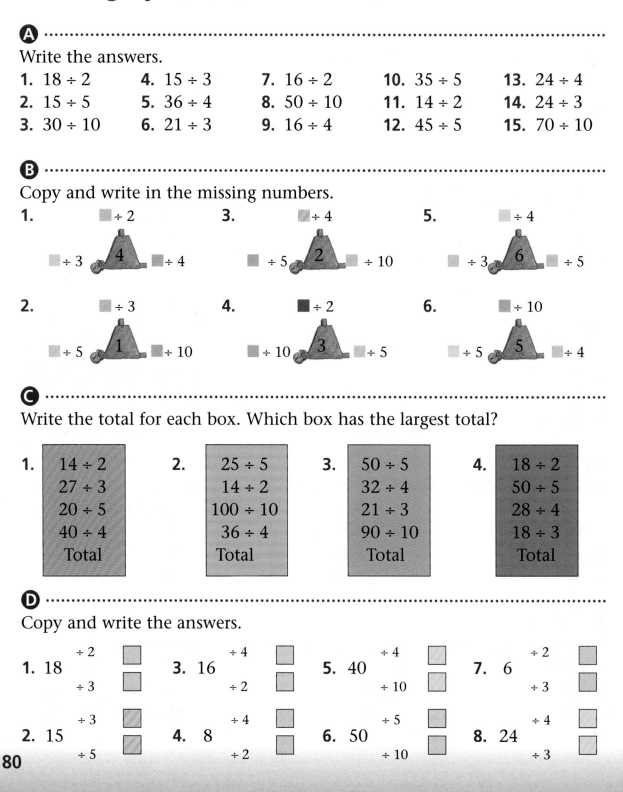

**1.** ■ ÷ 2   ■ ÷ 3   4   ■ ÷ 4

**3.** ■ ÷ 4   ■ ÷ 5   2   ■ ÷ 10

**5.** ■ ÷ 4   ■ ÷ 3   6   ■ ÷ 5

**2.** ■ ÷ 3   ■ ÷ 5   1   ■ ÷ 10

**4.** ■ ÷ 2   ■ ÷ 10   3   ■ ÷ 5

**6.** ■ ÷ 10   ■ ÷ 5   5   ■ ÷ 4

**C**

Write the total for each box. Which box has the largest total?

**1.**
14 ÷ 2
27 ÷ 3
20 ÷ 5
40 ÷ 4
Total

**2.**
25 ÷ 5
14 ÷ 2
100 ÷ 10
36 ÷ 4
Total

**3.**
50 ÷ 5
32 ÷ 4
21 ÷ 3
90 ÷ 10
Total

**4.**
18 ÷ 2
50 ÷ 5
28 ÷ 4
18 ÷ 3
Total

**D**

Copy and write the answers.

**1.** 18   ÷ 2 ☐   ÷ 3 ☐

**3.** 16   ÷ 4 ☐   ÷ 2 ☐

**5.** 40   ÷ 4 ☐   ÷ 10 ☐

**7.** 6   ÷ 2 ☐   ÷ 3 ☐

**2.** 15   ÷ 3 ☐   ÷ 5 ☐

**4.** 8   ÷ 4 ☐   ÷ 2 ☐

**6.** 50   ÷ 5 ☐   ÷ 10 ☐

**8.** 24   ÷ 4 ☐   ÷ 3 ☐

# Summary for Unit 8

**A** ........................................................................................................................

Write the answers.

1. $4 \div 2$
2. $16 \div 2$
3. $12 \div 2$

Halve these.

4. 20
5. 10
6. 14

Write the missing number.

7. $\square \div 2 = 5$
8. $\square \div 2 = 7$
9. $\square \div 2 = 3$

**B** ........................................................................................................................

Divide each number by 5.

1. 20
2. 45
3. 35

How many 5p coins in:

4. 15p
5. 30p
6. 45p

Write one-fifth of:

7. 10
8. 35
9. 20

**C** ........................................................................................................................

Write the answer.

1. $30 \div 10$
2. $80 \div 10$
3. $70 \div 10$

Divide by 10 and write the remainder.

4. 45
5. 63
6. 74

Write one-tenth of:

7. 60p
8. 80p
9. 40p

**D** ........................................................................................................................

Write one third of:

1. 15
2. 30
3. 24

Write the missing numbers.

4. $\square \div 3 = 4$
5. $\square \div 3 = 7$
6. $\square \div 3 = 5$

Divide by 3 and write the remainder.

7. 16
8. 20
9. 22

**E** ........................................................................................................................

Write how many fours in:

1. 28
2. 40
3. 36

Write one-quarter of:

4. 12
5. 24
6. 40

Write the totals.

7. $(12 \div 4) + (32 \div 4)$
8. $(16 \div 4) + (28 \div 4)$
9. $(36 \div 4) + (20 \div 4)$

# Helpful facts

## > < = symbols

> means is larger than: $\frac{1}{2} > \frac{1}{4}$

< means is smaller than: $\frac{1}{3} < \frac{1}{2}$

= means is equal to: $\frac{1}{2} = \frac{2}{4}$

## Equivalent fractions

Some fractions are worth the same even though they may look different:

$$\frac{1}{2} = \frac{2}{4} = \frac{3}{6} = \frac{4}{8}$$

$$\frac{1}{3} = \frac{2}{6} = \frac{3}{9} = \frac{4}{12}$$

$$\frac{1}{4} = \frac{2}{8} = \frac{3}{12} = \frac{4}{16}$$

$$\frac{1}{5} = \frac{2}{10} = \frac{3}{15} = \frac{4}{20}$$

## Equivalent strips

Equivalent strips help to compare fractions which are the same:

half
quarter
eighth
half
third
sixth
half
fifth
tenth

## Fractions of quantities

$\frac{1}{2}$ is the same as ÷ 2

$\frac{1}{4}$ is the same as ÷ 4

$\frac{1}{3}$ is the same as ÷ 3

# Learning outcomes for Unit 9

✓ recognise simple fractions, e.g. $\frac{1}{2}$, $\frac{1}{3}$, $\frac{1}{4}$

✓ recognise fractions of regular shapes

✓ recognise fractions of simple shapes

✓ estimate fractions of irregular shapes

✓ find simple fractions of quantities

✓ know equivalences of simple fractions, e.g. $\frac{1}{2} = \frac{2}{4}$

✓ compare and order simple fractions, e.g. $\frac{1}{2} > \frac{1}{3}$ $\frac{1}{4} < \frac{1}{3}$

# Simple Fractions of Shapes

**A** ....................................................................................................

Write whether each coloured part is one-half,
one-quarter or one-third of the whole shape.

1.       2.       3.       4.       5.       6.

**B** ....................................................................................................

Write whether each coloured part is $\frac{1}{2}$, $\frac{1}{4}$ or $\frac{1}{3}$ of the whole shape.

1.       2.       3.       4.       5.       6.

**C** ....................................................................................................

Write what fraction is coloured in.

1.       2.       3.       4.       5.       6.

**D** ....................................................................................................

Estimate whether $\frac{1}{2}$, $\frac{1}{4}$ or $\frac{1}{3}$ is coloured in.

1.       2.       3.       4.       5.       6.

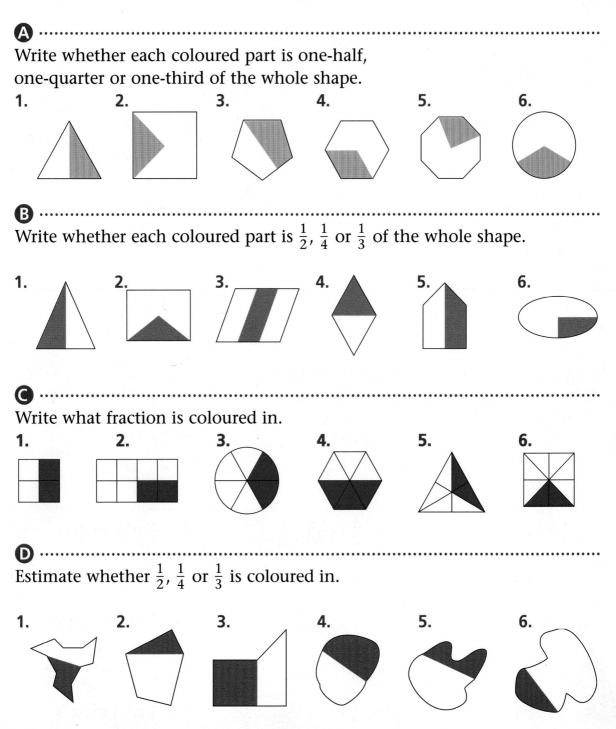

## Simple Fractions of Quantities

**A**

Find one-half of these quantities.

**1.** 8 scarves

**2.** 4 gloves

**3.** 20 hats

**4.** 12 T-shirts

**5.** 14 shirts

**6.** 6 belts

**B**

Find one-quarter of these amounts.

**1.** 8p

**2.** 24p

**3.** 36p

**4.** 12p

**5.** 16p

**6.** 28p

**7.** 20p

**8.** 32p

**9.** 40p

**C**

One-third is cut from each piece of ribbon.
Write how much is cut from each length.

**1.** 6 cm

**2.** 15 cm

**3.** 9 cm

**4.** 12 cm

**5.** 21 cm

**6.** 18 cm

**7.** 30 cm

**8.** 24 cm

**9.** 27 cm

**D**

**1.** $\frac{1}{3}$ of 18

**2.** $\frac{1}{2}$ of 16

**3.** $\frac{1}{3}$ of 21

**4.** $\frac{1}{4}$ of 16

**5.** $\frac{1}{4}$ of 24

**6.** $\frac{1}{2}$ of £14

**7.** $\frac{1}{3}$ of £30

**8.** $\frac{1}{2}$ of £20

**9.** $\frac{1}{4}$ of £40

**10.** $\frac{1}{3}$ of £24

**11.** $\frac{1}{4}$ of 8 metres

**12.** $\frac{1}{2}$ of 10 metres

**13.** $\frac{1}{4}$ of 12 metres

**14.** $\frac{1}{3}$ of 15 metres

**15.** $\frac{1}{2}$ of 6 metres

# Equivalence of Simple Fractions

**A**

Write pairs of fractions which are equivalent.

1. 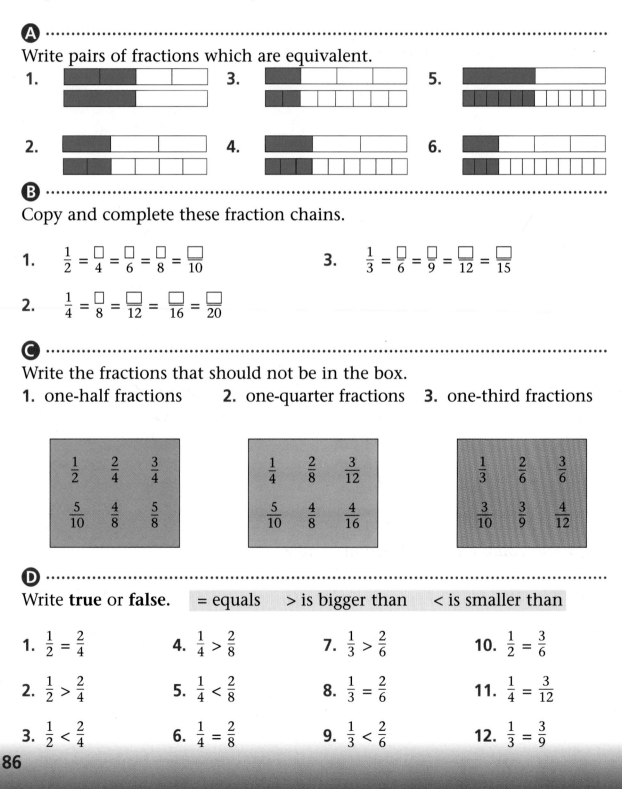  3.  5.

2.  4.  6.

**B**

Copy and complete these fraction chains.

1. $\dfrac{1}{2} = \dfrac{\square}{4} = \dfrac{\square}{6} = \dfrac{\square}{8} = \dfrac{\square}{10}$

3. $\dfrac{1}{3} = \dfrac{\square}{6} = \dfrac{\square}{9} = \dfrac{\square}{12} = \dfrac{\square}{15}$

2. $\dfrac{1}{4} = \dfrac{\square}{8} = \dfrac{\square}{12} = \dfrac{\square}{16} = \dfrac{\square}{20}$

**C**

Write the fractions that should not be in the box.

**1.** one-half fractions   **2.** one-quarter fractions   **3.** one-third fractions

| | | |
|---|---|---|
| $\dfrac{1}{2}$ | $\dfrac{2}{4}$ | $\dfrac{3}{4}$ |
| $\dfrac{5}{10}$ | $\dfrac{4}{8}$ | $\dfrac{5}{8}$ |

| | | |
|---|---|---|
| $\dfrac{1}{4}$ | $\dfrac{2}{8}$ | $\dfrac{3}{12}$ |
| $\dfrac{5}{10}$ | $\dfrac{4}{8}$ | $\dfrac{4}{16}$ |

| | | |
|---|---|---|
| $\dfrac{1}{3}$ | $\dfrac{2}{6}$ | $\dfrac{3}{6}$ |
| $\dfrac{3}{10}$ | $\dfrac{3}{9}$ | $\dfrac{4}{12}$ |

**D**

Write **true** or **false**.   = equals   > is bigger than   < is smaller than

1. $\dfrac{1}{2} = \dfrac{2}{4}$

4. $\dfrac{1}{4} > \dfrac{2}{8}$

7. $\dfrac{1}{3} > \dfrac{2}{6}$

10. $\dfrac{1}{2} = \dfrac{3}{6}$

2. $\dfrac{1}{2} > \dfrac{2}{4}$

5. $\dfrac{1}{4} < \dfrac{2}{8}$

8. $\dfrac{1}{3} = \dfrac{2}{6}$

11. $\dfrac{1}{4} = \dfrac{3}{12}$

3. $\dfrac{1}{2} < \dfrac{2}{4}$

6. $\dfrac{1}{4} = \dfrac{2}{8}$

9. $\dfrac{1}{3} < \dfrac{2}{6}$

12. $\dfrac{1}{3} = \dfrac{3}{9}$

# Summary for Unit 9

**A**
Write what fraction of each shape is coloured.

1. 

4. 

7. 

2. 

5. 

8. 

3. 

6. 

9. 

**B**

Find $\frac{1}{2}$ of:
1. 12
2. £6
3. 4 cm
4. 20p

Find $\frac{1}{3}$ of:
5. 21
6. 30p
7. 12 metres
8. £15

Find $\frac{1}{4}$ of:
9. 16
10. £20
11. 32 cm
12. 40p

**C**
Copy and complete these fraction families.

**1. Half Family**

$$\frac{\square}{4} \quad \frac{\square}{8} \quad \frac{\square}{10}$$

**2. Third Family**

$$\frac{\square}{6} \quad \frac{\square}{9} \quad \frac{\square}{12}$$

**3. Quarter Family**

$$\frac{\square}{8} \quad \frac{\square}{12} \quad \frac{\square}{16}$$

**10**

*Simple Decimals*

## Knowledge needed
✓ place value

# Helpful facts

## Decimal point
The decimal point separates:
- whole numbers from parts of numbers:
- pounds from pennies:

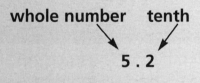

whole number    part of number

4 . 3

pounds    pence

£3 . 26

## Tenths
The decimal point comes between whole numbers and tenths:

whole number    tenth

5 . 2

## Halves
A half is the same as five tenths:

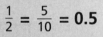

$\frac{1}{2} = \frac{5}{10} = 0.5$

# Learning outcomes for Unit 10

✓ know tenths as fractions and decimals

✓ recognise decimal notation in money

✓ recognise $\frac{1}{2}$ as decimal and fraction

✓ measure length in cm to one decimal place

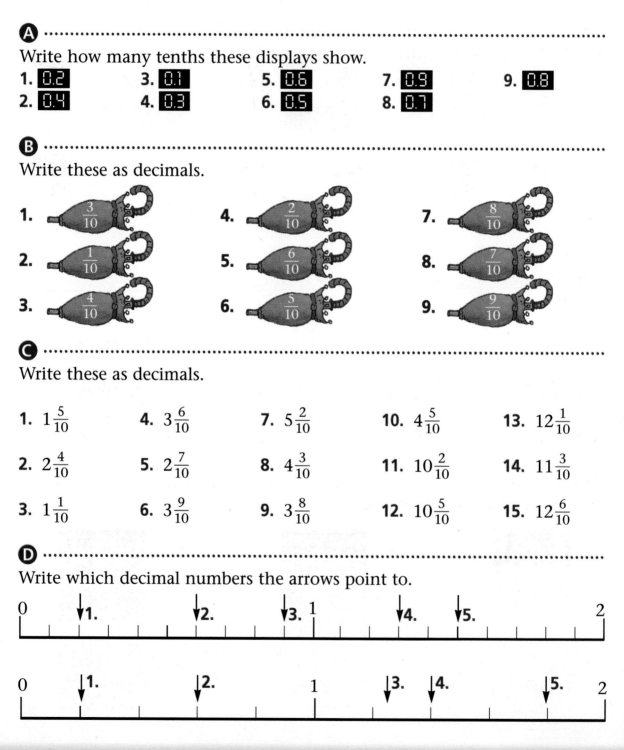

## 10.1

# Decimals and Tenths

**A**

Write how many tenths these displays show.
1. `0.2`      3. `0.1`      5. `0.6`      7. `0.9`      9. `0.8`
2. `0.4`      4. `0.3`      6. `0.5`      8. `0.7`

**B**

Write these as decimals.

1. $\frac{3}{10}$      4. $\frac{2}{10}$      7. $\frac{8}{10}$

2. $\frac{1}{10}$      5. $\frac{6}{10}$      8. $\frac{7}{10}$

3. $\frac{4}{10}$      6. $\frac{5}{10}$      9. $\frac{9}{10}$

**C**

Write these as decimals.

1. $1\frac{5}{10}$      4. $3\frac{6}{10}$      7. $5\frac{2}{10}$      10. $4\frac{5}{10}$      13. $12\frac{1}{10}$

2. $2\frac{4}{10}$      5. $2\frac{7}{10}$      8. $4\frac{3}{10}$      11. $10\frac{2}{10}$      14. $11\frac{3}{10}$

3. $1\frac{1}{10}$      6. $3\frac{9}{10}$      9. $3\frac{8}{10}$      12. $10\frac{5}{10}$      15. $12\frac{6}{10}$

**D**

Write which decimal numbers the arrows point to.

0 ↓1. ↓2. ↓3. 1 ↓4. ↓5. 2

0 ↓1. ↓2. 1 ↓3. ↓4. ↓5. 2

90

# Decimals and Money

**A** ................................................................................

Write how much each pile of money is worth.

**1.**  £1    10p

£ [ . ]

**3.**  £1    10p

£ [ . ]

**5.**  £1    10p

£ [ . ]

**2.**  £1    10p

£ [ . ]

**4.**  £1    10p

£ [ . ]

**6.**  £1    10p

£ [ . ]

**B** ................................................................................

Write how many pennies are in these amounts.

**1.** £0.50      **5.** £0.80      **9.** £0.65      **13.** £0.23

**2.** £0.40      **6.** £0.75      **10.** £0.15      **14.** £0.62

**3.** £0.30      **7.** £0.45      **11.** £0.67      **15.** £0.76

**4.** £0.60      **8.** £0.35      **12.** £0.51      **16.** £0.04

**C** ................................................................................

Write how much is in each box.

**1.**
£5 £1
50p

**3.**
£5 £1
£1 £1
10p 20p
20p 5p

**5.**
£5 £10
£1   2p
10p 10p

**2.**
£5 £1
£1 50p
20p

**4.**
£5 £10
10p

**6.**
£10 £10
50p 1p

# Decimals and Length

Estimate the length of each straw in cm.

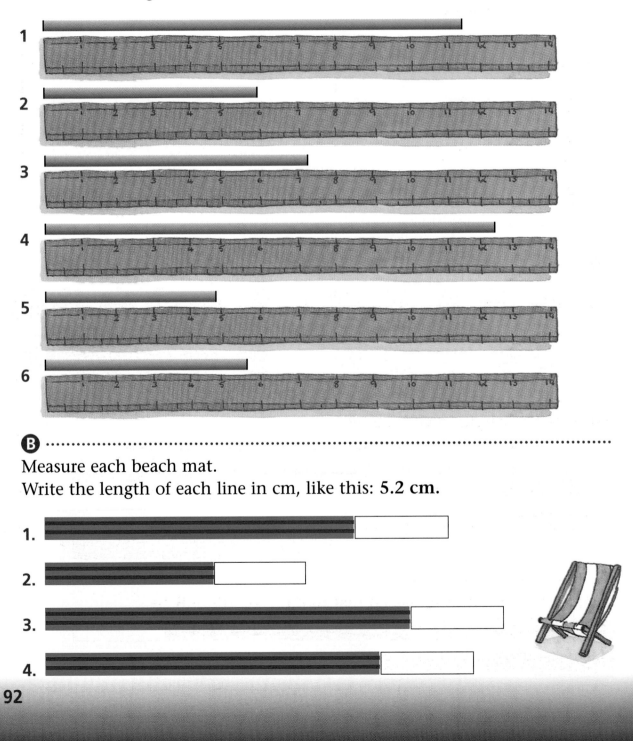

**B**

Measure each beach mat.
Write the length of each line in cm, like this: **5.2 cm.**

# Summary for Unit 10

**A** ...................................................................................................................

Write as decimals.

**1.** $2\frac{4}{10}$

**2.** $3\frac{7}{10}$

**3.** $1\frac{9}{10}$

**4.** $4\frac{1}{10}$

Write as tenths.

**5.** 0.4

**6.** 0.6

**7.** 0.2

**8.** 0.7

Write the number each arrow points to.

**9.**

**10.**

**11.**

**12.**

**B** ...................................................................................................................

Write how much each totals.

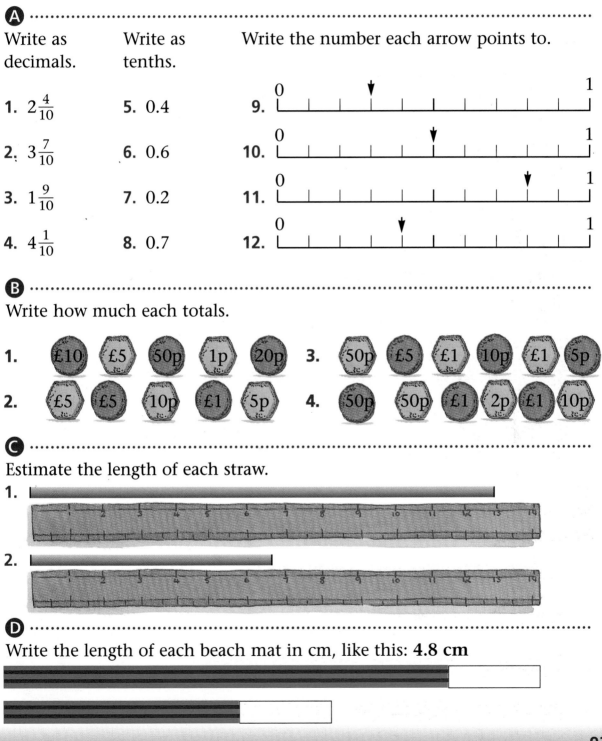

**1.** £10  £5  50p  1p  20p

**2.** £5  £5  10p  £1  5p

**3.** 50p  £5  £1  10p  £1  5p

**4.** 50p  50p  £1  2p  £1  10p

**C** ...................................................................................................................

Estimate the length of each straw.

**1.**

**2.**

**D** ...................................................................................................................

Write the length of each beach mat in cm, like this: **4.8 cm**

# Answers

**page 28** . . . . . . . . . . . . . . . . . . . . . . . . . . . . . . . . . . . . . . . . . . . . . . . . . . . . . . . . . . . . . . . . .

| 1. 9 | 3. 7 | 5. 7 | 7. 7 | 9. 9 |
| 2. 10 | 4. 8 | 6. 8 | 8. 9 | 10. 9 |

**page 29** . . . . . . . . . . . . . . . . . . . . . . . . . . . . . . . . . . . . . . . . . . . . . . . . . . . . . . . . . . . . . . . . .

| 1. 16 | 3. 14 | 5. 16 | 7. 16 | 9. 20 |
| 2. 14 | 4. 14 | 6. 15 | 8. 17 | 10. 19 |

**page 34** . . . . . . . . . . . . . . . . . . . . . . . . . . . . . . . . . . . . . . . . . . . . . . . . . . . . . . . . . . . . . . . . .

| 1. 9 | 3. 9 | 5. 7 | 7. 7 | 9. 6 |
| 2. 5 | 4. 9 | 6. 10 | 8. 7 | 10. 10 |

**page 35** . . . . . . . . . . . . . . . . . . . . . . . . . . . . . . . . . . . . . . . . . . . . . . . . . . . . . . . . . . . . . . . . .

| 1. 14 | 3. 17 | 5. 13 | 7. 11 | 9. 14 |
| 2. 12 | 4. 11 | 6. 18 | 8. 14 | 10. 16 |

**page 36** . . . . . . . . . . . . . . . . . . . . . . . . . . . . . . . . . . . . . . . . . . . . . . . . . . . . . . . . . . . . . . . . .

| 1. 4 | 3. 8 | 5. 5 | 7. 6 | 9. 1 |
| 2. 7 | 4. 10 | 6. 3 | 8. 2 | 10. 9 |

**page 37** . . . . . . . . . . . . . . . . . . . . . . . . . . . . . . . . . . . . . . . . . . . . . . . . . . . . . . . . . . . . . . . . .

| 1. 16 | 3. 14 | 5. 14 | 7. 50 | 9. 120 |
| 2. 13 | 4. 12 | 6. 60 | 8. 150 | 10. 120 |

**page 38** . . . . . . . . . . . . . . . . . . . . . . . . . . . . . . . . . . . . . . . . . . . . . . . . . . . . . . . . . . . . . . . . .

| 1. 70 | 3. 60 | 5. 80 | 7. 70 | 9. 80 |
| 2. 60 | 4. 80 | 6. 70 | 8. 80 | 10. 90 |

**page 39** . . . . . . . . . . . . . . . . . . . . . . . . . . . . . . . . . . . . . . . . . . . . . . . . .

| | | | | |
|---|---|---|---|---|
| **1.** 16 | **3.** 13 | **5.** 18 | **7.** 80 | **9.** 140 |
| **2.** 16 | **4.** 15 | **6.** 80 | **8.** 140 | **10.** 140 |

**page 40** . . . . . . . . . . . . . . . . . . . . . . . . . . . . . . . . . . . . . . . . . . . . . . . . .

| | | | | |
|---|---|---|---|---|
| **1.** 60 | **3.** 80 | **5.** 95 | **7.** 76 | **9.** 110 |
| **2.** 110 | **4.** 98 | **6.** 152 | **8.** 153 | **10.** 125 |

**page 49** . . . . . . . . . . . . . . . . . . . . . . . . . . . . . . . . . . . . . . . . . . . . . . . . .

| | | | | |
|---|---|---|---|---|
| **1.** 3 | **3.** 7 | **5.** 6 | **7.** 9 | **9.** 14 |
| **2.** 3 | **4.** 8 | **6.** 9 | **8.** 4 | **10.** 14 |

**page 54** . . . . . . . . . . . . . . . . . . . . . . . . . . . . . . . . . . . . . . . . . . . . . . . . .

| | | | | |
|---|---|---|---|---|
| **1.** 2 | **3.** 3 | **5.** 1 | **7.** 3 | **9.** 0 |
| **2.** 4 | **4.** 4 | **6.** 1 | **8.** 4 | **10.** 3 |

**page 56** . . . . . . . . . . . . . . . . . . . . . . . . . . . . . . . . . . . . . . . . . . . . . . . . .

| | | | | |
|---|---|---|---|---|
| **1.** 5 | **3.** 6 | **5.** 2 | **7.** 2 | **9.** 3 |
| **2.** 1 | **4.** 3 | **6.** 5 | **8.** 2 | **10.** 3 |

**page 57** . . . . . . . . . . . . . . . . . . . . . . . . . . . . . . . . . . . . . . . . . . . . . . . . .

| | | | |
|---|---|---|---|
| **1.** 8 | **3.** 4 | **5.** 5 | **7.** 6 |
| **2.** 4 | **4.** 2 | **6.** 7 | **8.** 3 |

**page 58** . . . . . . . . . . . . . . . . . . . . . . . . . . . . . . . . . . . . . . . . . . . . . . . . .

| | | | | |
|---|---|---|---|---|
| **1.** 6 | **3.** 4 | **5.** 2 | **7.** 20 | **9.** 30 |
| **2.** 0 | **4.** 1 | **6.** 30 | **8.** 50 | **10.** 40 |

# Detailed Topic Guide